The mutt Book

Decode Your Dog's Heritage

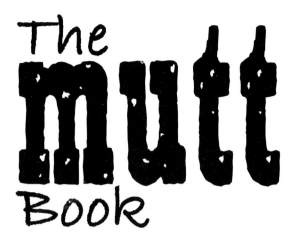

The mutt Book

Decode Your Dog's Heritage

David Alderton
foreword by Bruce Fogle

COLLINS & BROWN

First published in the United Kingdom in 2007 by
Collins & Brown
10 Southcombe Street
London
W14 0RA

An imprint of Anova Books Company Ltd

Produced by Hylas Publishing, 129 Main Street, Irvington, NY, 10533, USA

Hylas Publishing
Editor: Beth Adelman
Project Manager: Amber Rose
Senior Designers: Brian MacMullen, Gus Yoo
Designers: Lee Bartow, Ken Crossland, Erika Lubowicki
Photographer: Marc Henrie

ISBN 978-1-84340-393-7

A CIP catalogue for this book is available from the British Library.

9 8 7 6 5 4 3 2 1

Printed and bound by Star Standard Industries, Singapore

This book can be ordered direct from the publisher.
Contact the marketing department, but try your bookshop first.

www.anovabooks.com

Contents

Why We Love Them
by Bruce Fogle

This much I know: during the time I've been a clinical veterinarian, and that's almost 40 years, no dog has been more upwardly mobile than the ubiquitous mutt. Once he was the poor man's dog, the 'cottager's dog', as he was called in Victorian England. Mutts were the result then, as they mostly still are now, of unauthorised alliances, the progeny of freethinking dogs who simply did as nature intended, rather than as we imposed.

The elevation of the mutt from mongrel, Heinz 57, bitser, batard, to star status, is a curious consequence of our evolving relationship with the natural world around us. In my early years as a vet, purebred dogs were simply too expensive for many people to buy. And when a breeder's purebred dog accidentally mated with a dog of another breed, the resulting crossbred pups were either

drowned at birth or given to dog shelters or dog pounds. Mutts were free of charge and instantly available – no questions asked. They were the pets of poor families or those who thought they might want a dog but didn't want one enough to spend money on it.

As spendable income became more available, some working class families moved on to purebred dogs. But something else quite curious also happened. The mutt started to become fashionable. I'll give you an analogy from veterinary medicine to explain why.

Up until the 1960s, when I was a veterinary student, veterinary medicine was a man's profession – a rural man's profession. In the 1970s, veterinary schools started accepting students according to merit, not sex. At the same time, students from an urban background started to apply and attend.

This had a profound effect on the ethos of veterinary medicine. When I studied – I shudder to think how mindless we all were then – we carried out weekly 'surgical exercises' on mutts provided by the local pound. In the 1970s, the influx of new students baulked at doing so. They just said, "No!" They brought a different culture to veterinary education, an urban and more empathetic culture, in which care and compassion were more important than weight-per-day-of-age and market prices. In this culture, a mutt had as much value as a dog show prize winner.

These new students brought with them thoughts and ideas that were starting to percolate through what, at the time, was only a small section of society. How are we treating the natural world around us? What are we doing to the natural world around us? How can it be true that only humans have feelings and emotions while animals have just instincts? Are humans truly unique and separate from the rest of the animal world, or are we part of it?

Our rapidly changing attitude about the world around us affected our attitude towards our pets, and this was beneficial to mutts in three ways. First, dogs were seen as a respected species, as worthy of serious study as any other animal species. Second, mutts were considered by some as 'more natural' than purebreds, the result of natural selection rather than arbitrary human intervention. Some people involved in animal welfare were downright embarrassed to be seen in public with a purebred dog. (That was truly 'sleeping with the enemy'.) And third, mutts were seen as medically healthier than many purebreds, for it was rapidly emerging that, while creating breeds for specific looks and abilities, we had also unwittingly increased the incidence of specific inherited disorders in almost every breed – certainly in the breeds that were developed from a small gene pool.

I'm involved with Hearing Dogs for Deaf People, a charity that rescues young unwanted dogs from shelters and retrains them to act as ears for hearing-impaired people. Twenty-five years ago, we had no difficulty finding prospective Hearing Dogs. Shelters were bulging with little mutts. No longer. Today, we travel abroad to find the star mutts we need. We have to do so because people have become more responsible about caring for their dogs, so fewer of them end up in shelters, and because we have to compete with so many prospective dog owners who want to rescue a dog and give a mutt a good home. The reactive, alert, intelligent dogs we need are often gone the day they arrive.

The desire of so many families to have a mutt rather than a purebred is now so great that a new breeding industry has emerged: the intentional mutt, the crossbred breed, the 'designer dog', such as the Puggle, the Cockapoo, and the Labradoodle. I'm in favour. I'm in favour because crossbreeding dilutes potentially deleterious genes that adversely affect health, while still making it easy to guess the physical type and personality of the adult dog.

The advantage of knowing your mutt's background is that certain aspects of his behaviour are likely to be increased or diminished, based on the breeds that contributed to his mix. And that's where this book comes in. Because if you have a dog who's part terrier, you won't be surprised when he starts digging up the garden. A mutt with some sighthound in him is more likely to

chase the cat. And a shepherd mix will want to herd your kids.

The mutt's future? Who knows. Mutts are created by opportunist canines, but also by irresponsible dog owners. Forty years ago, the mutts I saw had terrier, hound or sheepdog ancestry. Today they are more likely to have Bull Terrier or Rottweiler ancestry. Creating mutts by crossing breeds? I'm in favour. After all, that's how most of the breeds of today were once developed. But irresponsible dog owners? When I'm in charge, I'll have them attend compulsory dog parenting classes and take exams before they can share their home with a dog.

Rescue Dogs: The Champions of Breeds

All readers of this book share a common love of dogs, and who can blame you? It's exceptionally rewarding to share our lives with dogs, and their reputation for loyalty, faithfulness and devotion is wholly deserved.

But have you ever wondered just where your pooch got those long legs, those crazy ears or that gorgeous, fluffy tail? Whether your dog is made up of two or twenty breeds, knowing who his ancestors were will give you much more than just a family tree. Finding out that your beloved dog is, in fact, part Retriever, has some Dachshund somewhere in his past, or is mainly made up of Terrier, will give you a much greater understanding of his personality – and his needs. Now you'll know why your dog keeps chasing squirrels or is so good at playing fetch! And if you find out that your dog is part Border Collie, you'll understand why he loves running around the countryside looking for sheep!

It's also the case that the more mixes of breeds your dog has, the more of an all-round great family pet he'll be! If his genetic make-up includes several breeds, the chances are he won't show any of the really distinct characteristics of a breed, but will simply be a wonderful all-round dog.

And of course, as you know, whether your dog is a pedigreed pooch or your average mixed-breed, every single

dog needs the same basic care, exercise, warmth, shelter, affection, love, understanding and respect. Sadly, not all dogs receive the care they deserve.

Hundreds of thousands of dogs are abandoned and unwanted every year. The lucky ones find themselves in rescue centres, from where they can find a new home and a second chance at happiness. Who could not be intensely moved by the fact that despite the poor start in life that so many of these dogs have had, their faith and trust is unswayed, their willingness to please is unchanged and above all, their love of people remains constant?

Is this enduring affection and loyalty not worth a hundred times more than the shape of a dog's head or the length of his legs?

This book will provide so much fun and entertainment, but more importantly, we hope it will instill and reinforce in us the respect for and understanding of dogs that they deserve. Their constant faith in us must not go unrewarded.

Clarissa Baldwin
Chief Executive, Dogs Trust

Dogs Trust is the UK's largest dog welfare charity and cares for around 14,000 dogs every year through its network of 17 Rehoming Centres across the UK. Dogs Trust never destroys a healthy dog, and its mission is to work towards the day when all dogs can enjoy a happy life, free from the threat of unnecessary destruction.

www.dogstrust.org.uk

Why Spay or Neuter Your Dog?

Thousands and thousands of dogs lose their lives each year because there aren't enough homes who want them and enough space in shelters to keep them. And it will always be so, as long as we keep breeding dogs casually.

Breeding dogs is a serious undertaking that should only be part of a well-planned programme. Why? Because dogs pass on their physical and behavioural problems to their offspring. Even healthy, well-behaved dogs can pass on genetic problems. It's a common misconception that mutts are free from the genetic defects that plague their purebred cousins. Yes, the larger the gene pool, the less chance that two mutant genes will randomly collide. But the fact is that mutts get all the diseases purebred dogs get. And just because a dog is healthy doesn't mean she doesn't have a defective gene lurking in her DNA.

Is your dog so sweet that you'd like to have a litter of puppies just like her? If only it were that easy! But if you breed her to another dog, the pups will not have the same genetic heritage she has. Let's face it: Most mutts are not the offspring of a clandestine liaison between two purebred dogs; rather, they're a mix of many, many crosses. How are you going to figure out the precise mix that produced her and then find a male who offers that exact same mix? It's impossible.

Breeding her *parents* again will increase the odds of a similar pup, but even then, the puppies in the second litter could inherit different genes. In fact, the only way to make a dog who is just like another dog, genetically speaking, is by cloning. And even then, the canine clone would be physically identical but behaviourally very different, because canine personalities, just like those of humans, are the result of complex interactions between genetics and environment.

What does this all mean? *There is no way to breed a dog who is just like another dog.* Each dog is a unique individual.

Plus, when you spay your female:
+ You avoid her heat cycles, during which she discharges blood and scent.
+ You greatly reduce her risk of developing mammary cancer and eliminate the risk of pyometra and uterine cancer.
+ You prevent unwanted pregnancies.

When you neuter your male:
+ You curb his desire to roam and to fight with other males.
+ You greatly reduce his risk of developing prostate cancer and eliminate the risk of testicular cancer.
+ You reduce his leg lifting and mounting behaviour.

World Map of Breeds

Hen and where dogs were first domesticated is still hotly debated, but there is no doubt that some breeds are very ancient. Variation in these dogs was probably due mostly to the variation in the wolves they descended from. But as domestic dogs travelled with their human companions, they adapted or were bred to suit the needs of the places and people around them. Some ancient types of domestic dogs died out, some survived and some contributed their genes to the development of the many breeds we see around the world today.

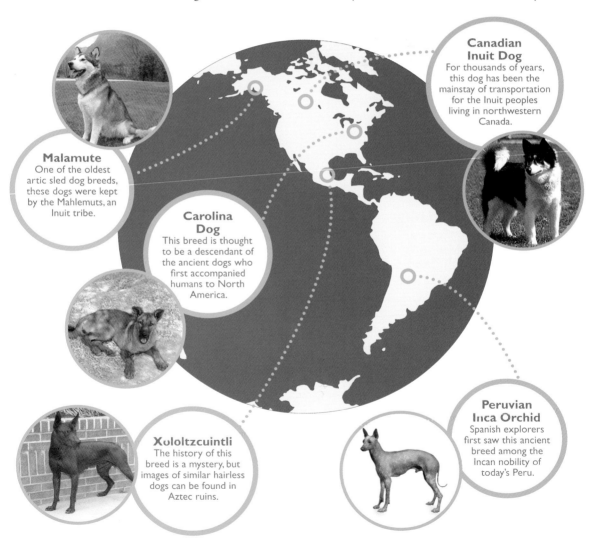

Canadian Inuit Dog
For thousands of years, this dog has been the mainstay of transportation for the Inuit peoples living in northwestern Canada.

Malamute
One of the oldest artic sled dog breeds, these dogs were kept by the Mahlemuts, an Inuit tribe.

Carolina Dog
This breed is thought to be a descendant of the ancient dogs who first accompanied humans to North America.

Xololtzcuintli
The history of this breed is a mystery, but images of similar hairless dogs can be found in Aztec ruins.

Peruvian Inca Orchid
Spanish explorers first saw this ancient breed among the Incan nobility of today's Peru.

Norwegian Buhund
A very old breed, the Buhund originally accompanied hunters and shepherds, and also pulled sleds.

Borzoi
The ancestors of this noble sighthound probably included hunting dogs used by Genghis Khan and the Mongol aristocracy.

Pug
The diminutive Pug was bred from larger dogs at least 2,400 years ago, to be the companion of Buddhist priests.

Irish Wolfhound
These big dogs from Ireland were admired as far away as ancient Rome for their size and nobility.

Ibizan Hound
Traders brought the Ibizan Hound to the Balearic Islands thousands of years ago, probably from Egypt.

Shiba Inu
The smallest and oldest of Japan's native breeds, his ancestors lived in mountain regions and hunted a variety of game.

Greyhound
Ancient carvings from the tomb of Amten in Egypt (built in the early third millennium BCE) show Greyhounds, and the Roman poet Ovid described this breed around the time of Christ.

Australian Cattle Dog
Crosses between the native dingoes (a wild dog descended from the Asian wolf) and a variety of English working breeds produced these dogs in the 1800s.

Basenji
This dog resembles pictures on Egyptian tombs from the Fourth Dynasty. How he made his way to central Africa is a mystery.

How to Use This Book

Welcome to your mutt! This book will teach you how to appreciate your favorite furry friend in a way you've never been able to before: as the sum of his parts. The first thing to do is to learn what to look for, and Part 1 will teach you how to do just that. It may seem odd to divide your dog into body parts such as head, ears, legs and so forth, but that's the best way to get at your dog's history. When you recognise parts – tails, ears and so on – that look like your dog, look to see what types of dog have those same characteristics and what breeds might therefore be in his mix.

Once you're able to recognise all the parts of your dog, you can look through the second part of the book to learn how to apply your newfound talents of identification. Every mutt is, of course, completely individual, but these pages may help you figure out how the whole dog fits together. You should be well-prepared to turn to your own mutt next, capable of reconstructing his heritage!

The sections in Part 1 will give you specific information about the general types of heads, ears, bodies, paws and legs, tails and coat colours and patterns found on dogs.

It's not always easy to understand the special language used to describe canine characteristics, but these visual glossaries will make it all clear.

Here you'll find important information about the characteristics discussed on these pages.

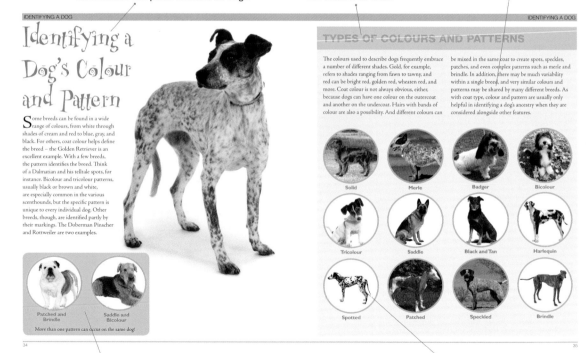

Identifying a Dog's Colour and Pattern

Some breeds can be found in a wide range of colours, from white through shades of cream and red to blue, gray, and black. For others, coat colour helps define the breed – the Golden Retriever is an excellent example. With a few breeds, the pattern identifies the breed. Think of a Dalmatian and his telltale spots, for instance. Bicolour and tricolour patterns, usually black or brown and white, are especially common in the various scenthounds, but the specific pattern is unique to every individual dog. Other breeds, though, are identified partly by their markings. The Doberman Pinscher and Rottweiler are two examples.

Patched and Brindle
Saddle and Bicolour
More than one pattern can occur on the same dog!

TYPES OF COLOURS AND PATTERNS

The colours used to describe dogs frequently embrace a number of different shades. Gold, for example, refers to shades ranging from fawn to tawny, and red can be bright red, golden red, wheaten red, and more. Coat colour is not always obvious, either, because dogs can have one colour on the outercoat and another on the undercoat. Hairs with bands of colour are also a possibility. And different colours can be mixed in the same coat to create spots, speckles, patches, and even complex patterns such as merle and brindle. In addition, there may be much variability within a single breed, and very similar colours and patterns may be shared by many different breeds. As with coat type, colour and pattern are usually only helpful in identifying a dog's ancestry when they are considered alongside other features.

Solid
Merle
Badger
Bicolour

Tricolour
Saddle
Black and Tan
Harlequin

Spotted
Patched
Speckled
Brindle

34

35

Look for the yellow box to find important distinctions among terms used to describe dogs.

Every dog here also appears on the following page – a gallery of some of the breeds who share each physical characteristic.

Since every mutt is an individual, we gave each dog his very own breed name – just for fun!

The big picture! Flip through the book to find a mutt like yours, or just enjoy the parade.

Look in the DOGnosis for the breeds that are likely to be in this mutt's ancestry. The bigger and darker the box, the stronger influence that breed had in this mutt's make-up.

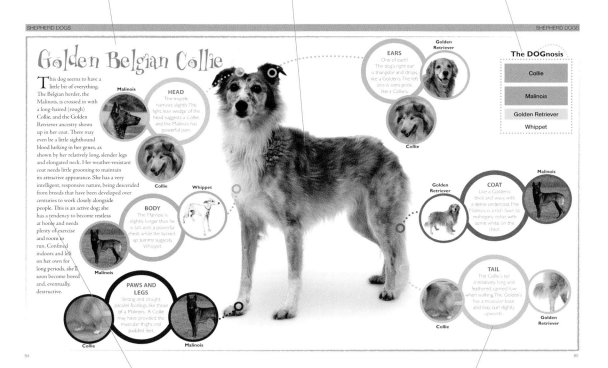

Here's some general information about what went into identifying this mutt's background, as well as some helpful clues about what you might expect in his behaviour and how much care he'll need.

These bubbles help explain why this mutt's parts suggest certain breeds. Accompanying pictures of the breeds bring it all into focus.

Part 1

Identifying a Dog

The best way to identify the breeds that are likely to be in your mutt's make-up is to look at his appearance. Sometimes he'll look a lot like one breed and much less like others but, because of random inheritances, this can be misleading. Better than trying to assess the whole is to look at individual parts. What you won't find here is a discussion of temperament. Generally speaking, terriers tend to be feisty, tenacious and curious. The shepherd breeds tend to be easy to train and good with families. The sighthounds are unreliable off leash, might chase other pets and are independent thinkers. The scenthounds are serious and vocal. The hunting dogs – spaniels, setters, retrievers and pointers – are active, alert and also good with families. But these are broad generalities. Each dog is an individual, and that is especially true when it comes to mutts. The best way to know a dog is to meet him – and to ask the shelter workers about him, as well. Never choose a dog on looks alone.

Identifying a Dog's Ear Shape

Wolves have prick ears, which are upright and triangular, and some breeds retain the ear shape of these original canine ancestors. Other breeds have ears that hang down, against the sides of the head. And still others have ear shapes somewhere between the two. Some dogs' ears hang down when they are relaxed but are raised when they hear interesting sounds. Dogs can also swivel their ears like radar dishes to follow sounds. When you look at your dog's ears, don't just look at the size and shape. It's also important to see where they are located on his head.

TYPES OF EARS

A specific vocabulary has been developed to describe all the different ear types, but since many of these terms are based on everyday objects, it's not hard to figure out their meanings.

Some ear types are associated with a breed type. Hunting dogs, for instance, often have drop ears, which fold over close to the head and hang down, while terriers very frequently have button ears, which are small and fold forwards at the tips. However, some terriers have prick ears, which are also charac-teristic of shepherd dogs, so things are not always perfectly straightforward. Ear shape can also be de-ceptive in young dogs, because some breeds, such as German Shepherds, have ears that hang down or fold over when they are puppies but stand upright when they are adults.

Some mutts will have ears that are unique to them – an individual combination that isn't found on any breed. And if you have a particularly furry dog, you may have trouble even finding his ears!

Prick

Drop

Button

Hound

Semi-prick

Tulip

High Set
Ears above a dog's eye level are consid-ered high set.

Low Set
Ears that begin below a dog's eye level are low set.

Rose

Flying

A Gallery of Ears

There are many different ear types, and identifying which one (or ones!) your dog has can help you decipher his ancestry. Use this gallery to help you name your mutt's ears and see which breeds have similar ones, but keep in mind that within each category there are many variations.

PRICK EARS

Australian Cattle Dog

Cairn Terrier

Chihuahua

Norwegian Buhund

DROP EARS

Saluki

Chesapeake Bay Retriever

Cocker Spaniel

Rhodesian Ridgeback

ROSE EARS

Greyhound

Whippet

TULIP EARS

French Bulldog

Corgi

HOUND EARS

Basset Hound

Beagle

Foxhound

Hamiltonstovare

FLYING EARS

Staffordshire Bull Terrier

SEMI-PRICK

Collie

Lakeland Terrier

BUTTON EARS

Border Terrier

Shar-Pei

Norfolk Terrier

Tibetan Spaniel

Identifying a Dog's Head

Head shapes can vary between extremes, from very narrow and elongated, like a Collie's, to short and round, like a Pug's. As with other body parts, features of a dog's head were developed with specific functions in mind, and therefore can be helpful in determining your mutt's ancestry. For instance, eyes which are placed close together, along with a slender muzzle, suggest a sighthound ancestor – these dogs hunt by tracking their prey visually, and that arrangement gives them great depth perception without obstructing their field of view. Wide, powerful jaws, and the wide skull needed to support them, are characteristic of dogs bred for guarding and similar duties.

TYPES OF HEADS

There are several parts of the head that are used to identify specific head types. The top of the head can be flat or domed, wide or narrow. The cheeks can be prominent or flat. The muzzle can be long or short, blunt or pointed. The flews (lips) can be tight or loose. The eyes can be big or small, set wide apart or close together. The place where the forehead ends and the muzzle begins – called the stop – can be either very pronounced (like a right angle), almost nonexistent or something in-between.

The terms used to describe head shape sometimes refer to other animals, such as foxes or otters. In other cases, they simply describe the appearance of the head, as in blocky, wedge-shaped, short or tapering. Dogs' heads can be described in profile, head-on or from the top.

Balanced

Blocky

Rectangular

Short

Fox-like

Otter

Tapering

Wedge-shaped

Squared-off Muzzle
The muzzle is strong and ends in a flat plane.

Pointed Muzzle
The muzzle tapers to a point at the nose, like a fox.

A Gallery of Heads

There are many different ways of looking at a dog's head, and several parts of the head can reveal clues about your mutt's ancestry. Use this gallery to help you identify your mutt's head, but keep in mind that a dog can have a hound muzzle and a hunting dog skull – or any other combination!

BALANCED

Airedale Terrier

Malinois

English Springer Spaniel

Golden Retriever

BLOCKY

Staffordshire Bull Terrier

Bulldog

Rhodesian Ridgeback

Rottweiler

FOX-LIKE

Finnish Lapphund

Shiba Inu

Keeshond

Pomeranian

OTTER

Border Terrier

TAPERING

Borzoi

Saluki

Whippet

RECTANGULAR

Irish Wolfhound

Scottish Terrier

Soft Coated Wheaten Terrier

Wire Fox Terrier

SHORT

Bulldog

Pug

French Bulldog

Tibetan Spaniel

WEDGE-SHAPED

Finnish Spitz

Collie

Australian Shepherd

Doberman Pinscher

Identifying a Dog's Body Shape

You can pick up important clues to your mutt's origins by assessing her overall body shape. A deep chest, extending down to the level of the elbows, indicates good lung capacity and means this is a dog whose ancestors were designed to run and be active. A more rotund shape is associated with a less athletic lifestyle. A broad chest is a sign of strength, and is characteristic of sled dogs, guard dogs and other breeds for whom power is important. There are even a few breeds, such as Dachshunds, whose unusual body shape was developed for a very specific purpose – in their case, hunting badgers in underground burrows.

TYPES OF BODIES

When you look at a dog's body in profile, it has an overall shape, composed of several important characteristics. For example, it may be square, rectangular, or long and, depending on the length of the legs, the dog may be tall or short. The underside may curve up under the tummy – called a tuck-up. The chest may curve down from the body. The topline may be level, slope towards the rump or dip a bit at the top of the shoulders. Head-on, the body might be broad or lithe, massive and blocky or light and elegant. Overall body type certainly tells you what work this dog was bred to do. When you look at your dog, ask yourself: Does this look like the body of a runner, a guardian, a hunter or simply a companion?

Deep Chest

Broad Chest

Massive/blocky

Lithe

Square

Long

Rectangular

Tuck-up

Tall

Short

Level Topline
The back is perfectly sraight and level.

Sloping Topline
This topline slopes away at the rump.

A Gallery of Body Shapes

There are many different body types, and identifying which one your dog has can help you understand what kind of job your dog was meant to do. Use this gallery to help you name your mutt's body type and see which breeds look similar, but keep in mind that within each category there are many variations.

RECTANGULAR

Beauceron

Scottish Deerhound

Greyhound

TUCK-UP

Borzoi

Greyhound

Saluki

Whippet

SQUARE

Brittany

French Bulldog

Pug

LONG

Dachshund

Corgi

Dandie Dinmont Terrier

DEEP CHEST

Pointer

Doberman Pinscher

Beauceron

Rhodesian Ridgeback

BROAD CHEST

Bulldog

Malamute

Labrador Retriever

Rottweiler

SHORT

Cairn Terrier

Yorkshire Terrier

TALL

Great Dane

Irish Wolfhound

MASSIVE/BLOCKY

Staffordshire Bull Terrier

Bulldog

Bullmastiff

Shar-Pei

LITHE

Ibizan Hound

Saluki

Whippet

Identifying a Dog's Coat

Long, short, soft or wiry – there are a number of different possible combinations for coats. There are even a few breeds with very little hair at all. Coat type sometimes tells you a lot – as with terriers, many of whom have distinctive wiry coats, and northern breeds, who have thick, plush double coats. But sometimes coat type can be deceptive, because a few breeds, such as the Dachshund, have been developed in longhaired, shorthaired and wirecoated variations. It's also true that a mutt may show the coat characteristics of several of his ancestors.

Double Coat
Most dogs have a short, soft undercoat and a longer outercoat.

Single Coat
Some breeds have just a single, short coat. To check, part the dog's fur.

Types of Coats

While you can often assess the coat texture simply from a dog's appearance, you may need to part the fur on some dogs to see whether, for example, there is a dense undercoat close to the skin. Coat length is often a clue to ancestry, but the length of the coat is not necessarily consistent over the entire body. The fur is often shorter on the face than elsewhere and sometimes longer on the legs and tail, a feature called feathering.

The coat contributes greatly to the overall look of the dog, and often we are tempted to choose a dog on looks alone. But in the long run, personality is far more important than looks when you're considering a new pet.

Bristle **Close** **Single** **Double**

Crinkly **Curly** **Smooth** **Glossy**

Stand-off **Thick** **Wire**

A Gallery of Coats

We tend to think of canine coats as just short or long, but there are many variations on that theme. Identifying your dog's coat type will tell you something about the part of the world he came from and the work he was bred to do. Use this gallery to help you name your mutt's coat type and find breeds with a similar coat. Remember, however, that there is a lot of variability in each category and that mutts may show coat traits inherited from several of their ancestors at once.

BRISTLE

Shar-Pei

Shiba Inu

CRINKLY

Wire Fox Terrier

Airedale Terrier

CLOSE

Staffordshire Bull Terrier

Australian Cattle Dog

Greyhound

Whippet

CURLY

Irish Water Spaniel

Standard Poodle

DOUBLE

Akita

Bearded Collie

GLOSSY

Chihuahua

Dalmatian

Flat-Coated Retriever

Manchester Terrier

SINGLE

Papillon

Miniature Pinscher

Weimaraner

Standard Poodle

SMOOTH

Basset Hound

Beagle

Boxer

Doberman Pinscher

STAND-OFF

Norweigan Elkhound

Keeshond

Pomeranian

Shiba Inu

THICK

Affenpinscher

Australian Shepherd

Labrador Retriever

Siberian Husky

WIRE

Irish Terrier

Norfolk Terrier

Border Terrier

Scottish Deerhound

Identifying a Dog's Colour and Pattern

Some breeds can be found in a wide range of colours, from white through shades of cream and red to blue, grey, and black. For others, coat colour helps define the breed – the Golden Retriever is an excellent example. With a few breeds, the pattern identifies the breed. Think of a Dalmatian and his telltale spots, for instance. Bicolour and tricolour patterns, usually black or brown and white, are especially common in the various scenthounds, but the specific pattern is unique to every individual dog. Other breeds, though, are identified partly by their markings. The Doberman Pinscher and Rottweiler are two examples.

Patched and Brindle

Saddle and Bicolour

More than one pattern can occur on the same dog!

TYPES OF COLOURS AND PATTERNS

The colours used to describe dogs frequently embrace a number of different shades. Gold, for example, refers to shades ranging from fawn to tawny, and red can be bright red, golden red, wheaten red and more. Coat colour is not always obvious, either, because dogs can have one colour on the outercoat and another on the undercoat. Hairs with bands of colour are also a possibility. And different colours can be mixed in the same coat to create spots, speckles, patches and even complex patterns such as merle and brindle. In addition, there may be much variability within a single breed and very similar colours and patterns may be shared by many different breeds. As with coat type, colour and pattern are usually only helpful in identifying a dog's ancestry when they are considered alongside other features.

Solid

Merle

Badger

Bicolour

Tricolour

Saddle

Black and Tan

Harlequin

Spotted

Patched

Speckled

Brindle

A Gallery of Colours and Patterns

Dogs come in an almost infinite array of colours and patterns. Sometimes they tell us a great deal about a mutt's ancestry, but sometimes they just help narrow things down a bit or even tell us almost nothing.

This gallery will help you name your mutt's pattern and show you which breeds have a similar look. Colour and patterns are some of the trickiest and most variable of features, so don't judge your dog by his coat alone!

MERLE

Australian Cattle Dog

BADGER

Petit Basset Griffon Vendeen

SOLID

Affenpinscher

Flat-Coated Retriever

Irish Terrier

Vizsla

BICOLOUR

Border Collie

Finnish Lapphund

Australian Terrier

Bearded Collie

TRICOLOUR

Basset Hound

Jack Russell Terrier

Greater Swiss Mountain Dog

Corgi

SADDLE

Airedale Terrier

German Shepherd

Welsh Terrier

HARLEQUIN

Great Dane

BLACK AND TAN

Beauceron

Manchester Terrier

Rottweiler

Doberman Pinscher

PATCHED

Ibizan Hound

Papillon

Cavalier King Charles Spaniel

Brittany

SPECKLED

German Shorthaired Pointer

English Setter

English Springer Spaniel

SPOTTED

Dalmatian

BRINDLE

Whippet

Greyhound

Identifying a Dog's Tail

All dogs use their tails to communicate their moods, and the special signals they send are the same for all types of dogs. But the shape and position of the tail can vary a great deal among the breeds. For example, hounds who hunt in packs, such as Beagles and Foxhounds, have straight tails that they carry upright, like a flag. In contrast, sighthounds carry their tails low, with either a gentle curve at the end or right between their legs. Most terriers have upright tails set high on their backs.

High Set
A tail that seems to be a natural extension of the topline is high set.

Low Set
A tail that begins below the topline is low set.

TYPES OF TAILS

The shape of the tail, its length and the way it is held will influence what it's called – and will give you a clue to your dog's heritage. The brush tail, for example, describes a heavily-furred tail. A sickle tail curves forwards over the back, and when you combine the two, you have a brush sickle tail – as on a Finnish Spitz. Curled tails are short with a twist in them, like a Pug's, while gay tails are held vertically, like a Wire Fox Terrier's. There are a few breeds, such as the Cardigan Welsh Corgi, which have very short bobtails; this is a natural genetic variation. Dogs with very short tails have been known to wag their whole back end when they're excited!

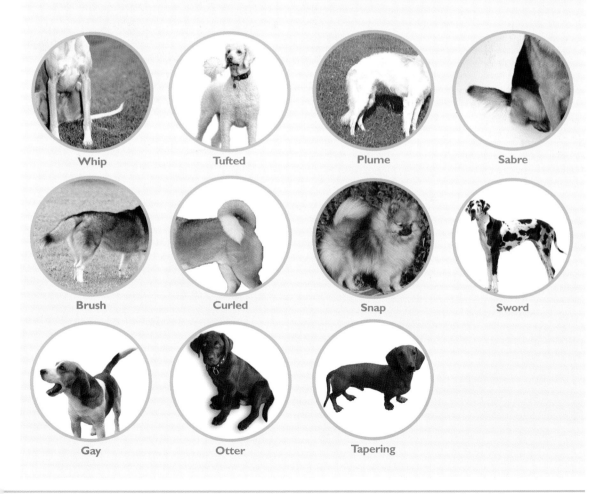

Whip

Tufted

Plume

Sabre

Brush

Curled

Snap

Sword

Gay

Otter

Tapering

A Gallery of Tails

There are many different types of tails, and sometimes more than one descriptive word will apply to the same tail. Use this gallery to help you name your mutt's tail type and see which breeds have similar tails. As always, there are many variations, and your mutt may have a tail all his own!

BRUSH

Siberian Husky

Finnish Spitz

OTTER

Chesapeake Bay Retriever   Labrador Retriever

CURLED

Akita

Pug

SWORD

Staffordshire Bull Terrier

Great Dane

Greater Swiss Mountain Dog

Pointer

SNAP

Malamute

Pomeranian

TUFTED

Standard Poodle   Miniature Poodle

GAY

Cavalier King Charles Spaniel

Beagle

German Shorthaired Pointer

Wire Fox Terrier

TAPERING

Dachshund

Manchester Terrier

Border Terrier

SABRE

German Shepherd

Petit Basset Griffon Vendeen

PLUME

Borzoi

Saluki

Tervuren

WHIP

Whippet

Ibizan Hound

Identifying a Dog's Paws and Legs

In addition to looking at the length and thickness of a dog's legs, the angle at which they join the body tells us a lot about the dog's athletic ability. The position of the legs is also influenced by the body shape; a broad-chested dog, for instance, is likely to have wide-set limbs. The shape of the paws also helps indicate what type of activity the dog was bred for. Northern breeds have thick, hard footpads, necessary for running on hard earth and snow, while webbing between the toes is common in breeds that work in water, such as Labrador Retrievers.

Long
Not all long-legged dogs are tall!

Short
Not all short-legged dogs are tiny!

TYPES OF PAWS AND LEGS

It's not just the length of a mutt's legs that is significant in terms of determining her possible ancestry, but also the shape. In some breeds, such as Basset Hounds and Bulldogs, the front legs are turned outwards. In other breeds, including many terriers, the front legs are perfectly straight, have a crisp bend at the wrist and end in paws that point straight ahead. There are a number of different paw shapes too; rounder paws provide strength and stability, while hare-shaped paws (long and narrow) are built for speed and typify some of the faster breeds (although many toy breeds have them too). Powerful muscles on the back legs suggest an ancestor bred for strength or speed, but these should be considered in combination with the mutt's general body shape.

PAWS

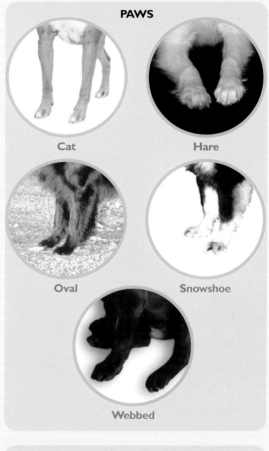

Cat

Hare

Oval

Snowshoe

Webbed

FRONT LEGS

Straight

Bowed

Bent (at wrist)

Wide-set

BACK LEGS

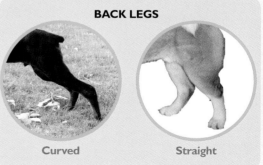

Curved

Straight

A Gallery of Paws and Legs

There are more types of paws and legs than you might think, and identifying which ones your dog has can give you clues to her background. Use this gallery to help you name your mutt's paws and legs and see which breeds are similar, but keep in mind that every category has many variations.

PAWS

CAT

Boxer

Miniature Pinscher

Cocker Spaniel

Beagle

HARE

Borzoi

Papillon

OVAL

Bearded Collie

Flat-Coated Retriever

SNOWSHOE

Finnish Lapphund

Malamute

Norwegian Elkhound

Siberian Husky

WEBBED

Chesapeake Bay Retriever

Labrador Retriever

BACK LEGS

CURVED

Brittany

Doberman Pinscher

STRAIGHT

Akita

Cairn Terrier

Finnish Lapphund

Smooth Fox Terrier

FRONT LEGS

STRAIGHT

English Springer Spaniel

Manchester Terrier

BOWED

Bulldog

Pug

BENT (AT WRIST)

Basset Hound

Dachshund

WIDE-SET

Bullmastiff

Great Dane

Part 2
David Alderton Identifies the Mutts

The best start to determining the likely origins of a mutt is to first consider his size and body shape. This will give you an initial overall impression of what kind of dog he is. You can then begin to look more carefully at individual aspects of his appearance – head shape, paws and legs, tail and so forth – in search of further clues about his ancestry. And do not forget that the dog's temperament and behaviour may provide you with additional insights. Even with all of this, though, figuring out a mutt's heritage is basically a series of educated guesses. But the effort will certainly teach you a lot about your dog!

Terrier Types

Affencairn

Affenpinscher

Clearly descended from terrier stock, this is a lively dog who would enjoy living in a suburban home with a garden and a park nearby for walks, but he would be equally at home in a more rural environment. His coat care is fairly straightforward, since, like most terriers, it is weather-resistant and needs relatively little grooming. In fact, the slightly unkempt appearance adds to his charm. He may, however, benefit from having his coat trimmed back every two or three months. If you're not ready to do that yourself, you may need to take him to a groomer. It is also important to make sure the longer hair around his mouth does not become soiled with food and dirt. You may need to wipe his beard every day, or he'll end up smelling unpleasant.

HEAD
The powerful, square muzzle is most likely from the Cairn Terrier, and the abundant mustache and beard is all Affenpinscher.

Cairn Terrier

Affenpinscher

PAWS AND LEGS
The overall stocky appearance and short legs are found in Cairn Terriers, whose front feet are slightly bigger than their back feet, and Affenpinschers, who have tight, round feet.

Cairn Terrier

EARS

Scottish Terrier

Pointed, well-spaced ears are a balance between the Scottish Terrier, who has bigger ears, and the Australian Terrier, whose ears are smaller.

Australian Terrier

The DOGnosis

Cairn Terrier
Affenpinscher
Scottish Terrier
Australian Terrier

Cairn Terrier

BODY

The powerful, rectangular body suggests the Cairn Terrier, who has a level back and deep ribs, or Australian Terrier, with his low-reaching chest.

Australian Terrier

COAT

The double coat, found on the Cairn Terrier and Affenpinscher, provides good protection against the elements.

Affenpinscher

Cairn Terrier

51

Smooth Boxfox Staffie

This dog is still growing up, but he is clearly a character. He also has the potential to become a difficult dog without adequate training, being quite strong-willed by nature. He is a terrier and is descended from the tough guys of the terrier group: most likely the Staffordshire Bull Terrier and the Smooth Fox Terrier. He is also likely to be rather territorial, and needs socialising with other dogs from an early age. Otherwise, he will not play well with others – especially those who do not recognise his tough-guy nature. On the other hand, the fearsome reputation of the Bull Terrier breeds is not entirely justified. These dogs can be trained well, and a number are used in hospital visiting programmes and other projects where they have close contact with strangers. Early socialisation will help, as will neutering him.

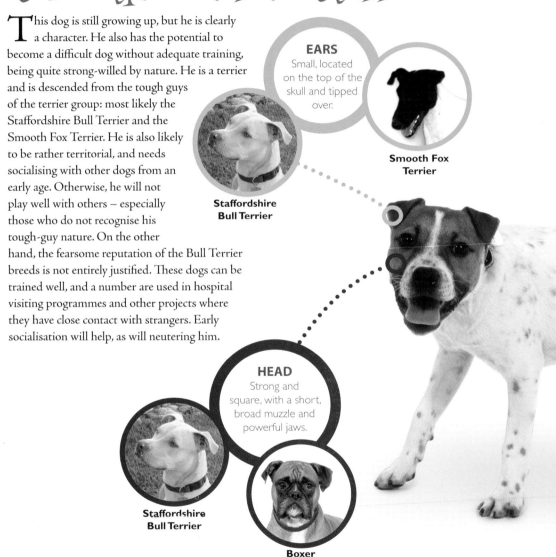

EARS
Small, located on the top of the skull and tipped over.

Smooth Fox Terrier

Staffordshire Bull Terrier

HEAD
Strong and square, with a short, broad muzzle and powerful jaws.

Staffordshire Bull Terrier

Boxer

Boxer

The DOGnosis

Staffordshire Bull Terrier
Boxer
Smooth Fox Terrier

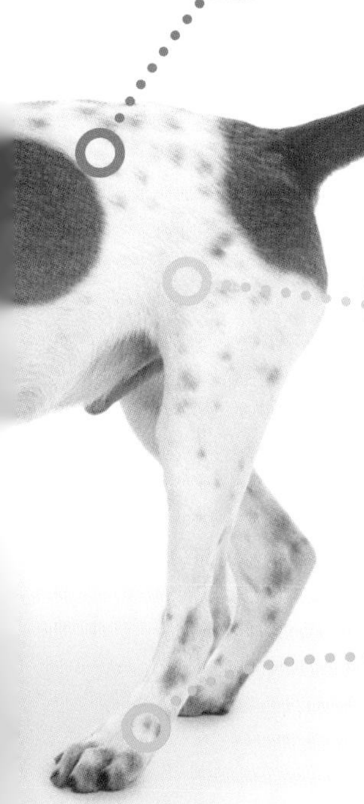

Staffordshire Bull Terrier

COAT
Glossy, stiff and short, like all three breeds. The colouring is most like that of a Fox Terrier, but can turn up on any of them.

Smooth Fox Terrier

Smooth Fox Terrier

BODY
Compact, muscular, with a deep, broad chest – tough terrier all the way.

Staffordshire Bull Terrier

PAWS AND LEGS
Absolutely straight front legs say Fox Terrier; powerful hind legs are a Staffie inheritance.

Smooth Fox Terrier

Staffordshire Bull Terrier

Wheatlake Terrier

This dog has an alert, curious nature with an independent streak that can hamper his training. He likes people but tends not to be very friendly towards other dogs. These traits give us a clue to his ancestry as a cross-bred terrier – which helps explain his tousled coat, the shape of his ears and the way he holds his tail. His colouration suggests that he has some Soft Coated Wheaten Terrier in his background; the breed has a softer coat than most terriers and it is the colour of ripening wheat. The other terriers in his background give this dog his long legs, fuzzy face and mischievous nature.

Irish Terrier

EARS
Set high and wide on the head, V-shaped and folded forward.

Wire Fox Terrier

Lakeland Terrier

PAWS AND LEGS
The beautiful, straight front legs are found on all of these terriers, while the round, compact feet are from the Wire Fox.

Wire Fox Terrier

Irish Terrier

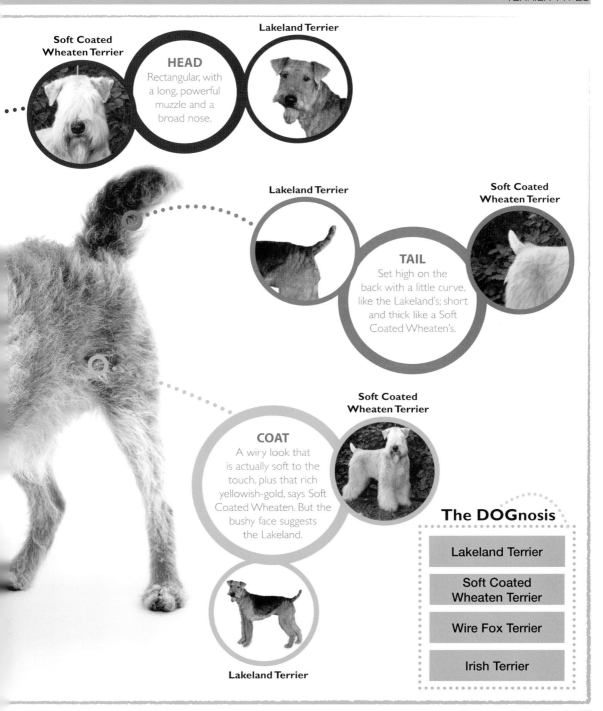

Soft Coated Wheaten Terrier

Lakeland Terrier

HEAD
Rectangular, with a long, powerful muzzle and a broad nose.

Lakeland Terrier

Soft Coated Wheaten Terrier

TAIL
Set high on the back with a little curve, like the Lakeland's; short and thick like a Soft Coated Wheaten's.

Soft Coated Wheaten Terrier

COAT
A wiry look that is actually soft to the touch, plus that rich yellowish-gold, says Soft Coated Wheaten. But the bushy face suggests the Lakeland.

Lakeland Terrier

The DOGnosis

Lakeland Terrier

Soft Coated Wheaten Terrier

Wire Fox Terrier

Irish Terrier

Northern Manfolk Terrier

HEAD
Tapers to a triangle, with a pointy muzzle and dark eyes.

Finnish Spitz

Shiba Inu

There is no doubt that this dog is descended, in part, from one of the northern breeds (also known as Spitz breeds), probably a Shiba Inu or a Finnish Spitz (depending on where she lives). She has some of the typical characteristics of those breeds, including a tail that curves over her back and a pointed, fox-like face. However, her folded-over ears and scruffy coat suggest some terrier in her make-up. So we could say this dog is a northern breed at both ends and a terrier in the middle. Certainly, she is responsive and friendly, although she can be noisy – a reflection of both her northern heritage and the instinctive alertness of a terrier.

PAWS AND LEGS
Short, straight legs, with compact, rounded feet – traits of both the Manchester and the Smooth Fox Terriers.

Manchester Terrier

Smooth Fox Terrier

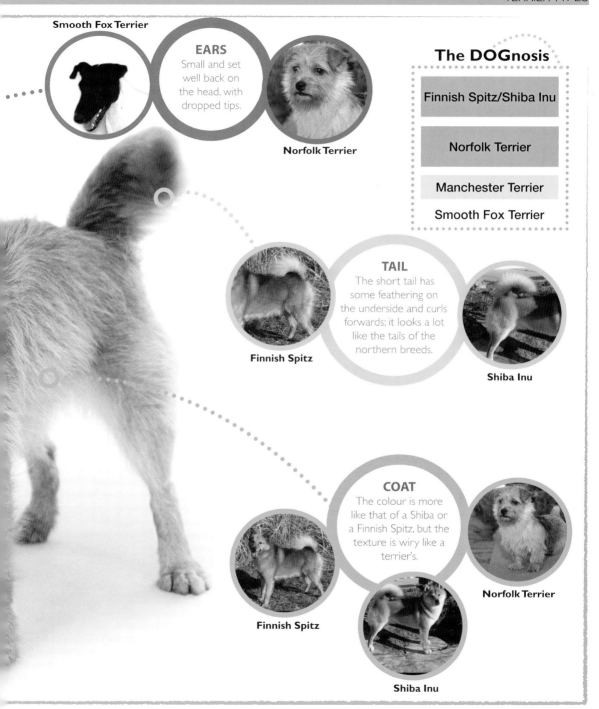

Smooth Fox Terrier

EARS
Small and set well back on the head, with dropped tips.

Norfolk Terrier

The DOGnosis

| Finnish Spitz/Shiba Inu |
| Norfolk Terrier |
| Manchester Terrier |
| Smooth Fox Terrier |

TAIL
The short tail has some feathering on the underside and curls forwards; it looks a lot like the tails of the northern breeds.

Finnish Spitz

Shiba Inu

COAT
The colour is more like that of a Shiba or a Finnish Spitz, but the texture is wiry like a terrier's.

Finnish Spitz

Norfolk Terrier

Shiba Inu

Dandie Border Scottie

A dog with an unmistakable terrier profile, his rather long face suggests a Scottish Terrier – but only in part. A little Dandie Dinmont Terrier in his ancestry would help to explain the folded ears, as well as the tuft on the top of his head. His colouration is also faintly reminiscent of a Dandie Dinmont – a mixture sometimes described as 'pepper-and-salt' – and his long, low body could be Cairn Terrier or more Dandie. Ever-alert and quite strong-willed (like all terriers), he loves investigating every hole in the ground. He is not deterred by bad weather, either, being well-protected from the elements by his wiry double coat.

Dandie Dinmont Terrier

BODY
Broad and close to the ground, like both the Dandie and Cairn, and long like a Dandie.

Cairn Terrier

TAIL
Short and thick, tapering to a point.

Border Terrier

Scottish Terrier

Scottish Terrier

HEAD
Broad at the top of the skull, with a short, wide muzzle.

Dandie Dinmont Terrier

COAT
Medium length and wiry like a Cairn; pepper-and-salt, hard-and-soft like a Dandie.

Dandie Dinmont Terrier

Cairn Terrier

PAWS AND LEGS
Short, straight legs suggest Dandie Dinmont, with the front feet bigger than the hind feet, as on a Border Terrier.

The DOGnosis

Scottish Terrier

Dandie Dinmont Terrier

Border Terrier

Cairn Terrier

Dandie Dinmont Terrier

Border Terrier

Norcairnshire Terrier

His broad face, folded ears, short legs and a coat that is longer over the shoulders than on the body are all clues that point to a Norfolk Terrier ances-tor. It's likely that the Border Terrier played a part too, with that large, round face. His coat is much less wiry than that of most terriers, suggesting there might be a little bit of Yorkie lurking here too. He is an active dog, keen to go out even when the weather is bad, trotting along rather than running – but certainly never walking slowly with those short legs. His coat is easy to keep clean; any dirt that sticks to it will soon dry and can then be easily brushed out.

Norfolk Terrier

HEAD
Broad and flat on top indicate Norfolk and Border Terriers, and the compact muzzle is Border all the way. The big, round eyes are like a Yorkie's.

Yorkshire Terrier

Border Terrier

PAWS AND LEGS
Short, with the front legs angled slightly forward like a Cairn's and well-angled at the rear, like a Norfolk's.

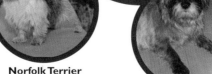

Norfolk Terrier

Cairn Terrier

EARS
Small and folded down by the sides of the head, like those of both the Border and Norfolk Terriers.

Norfolk Terrier

Border Terrier

The DOGnosis

Norfolk Terrier
Border Terrier
Cairn Terrier
Yorkshire Terrier

Norfolk Terrier

COAT
Scruffy and reddish, like a typical Norfolk, but not harsh to the touch, like a Yorkie.

Yorkshire Terrier

Cairn Terrier

BODY
Longer than he is tall, like a Norfolk, with a deep chest like a Cairn.

Norfolk Terrier

Welman Terrier

There is little doubt that this dog is another descendant of terrier stock. In the past, there was a different terrier type for almost every town and village. But nowadays there's a lot of intermingling. And all terriers everywhere have certain characteristics that can be recognized right away: the squarish muzzle with a beard underneath, the wiry coat, the strong back and chest, the tail that's short but not stubby. This lively terrier is still young, but you can see even now that she will develop into a solidly built adult. Her intense, curious expression is also pure terrier. Tenacious and energetic, this dog needs a lot of activity to keep her from becoming yappy and destructive, and will love poking her nose into every available hole.

Manchester Terrier

HEAD
The head narrows slightly (like a Manchester's) down to the square muzzle (like a Welsh Terrier's).

Welsh Terrier

COAT
Wiry and thick at the beard and chest, like the Welsh Terrier. Her colour suggests the black and tan of the Manchester.

Manchester Terrier

Welsh Terrier

Manchester Terrier

PAWS AND LEGS
Long, strong, straight legs are from the Manchester, and her height suggests some Airedale.

Airedale Terrier

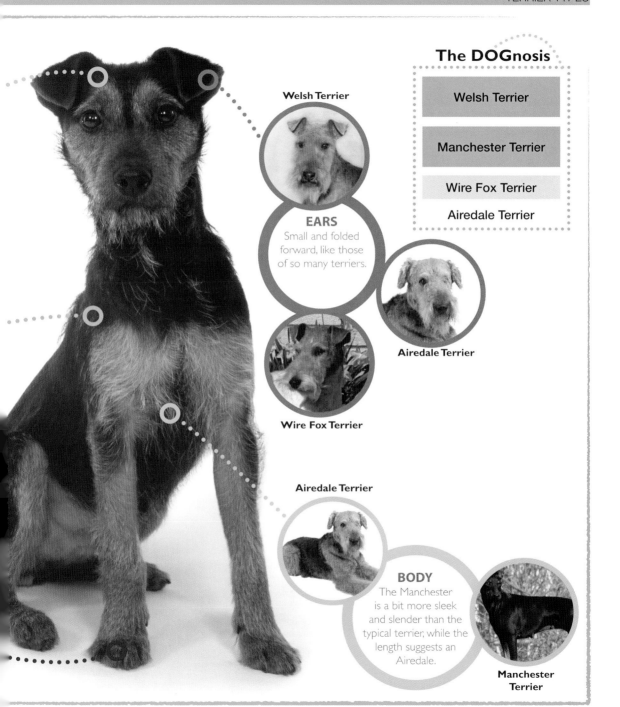

Welsh Terrier

The DOGnosis

Welsh Terrier

Manchester Terrier

Wire Fox Terrier

Airedale Terrier

EARS
Small and folded forward, like those of so many terriers.

Airedale Terrier

Wire Fox Terrier

Airedale Terrier

BODY
The Manchester is a bit more sleek and slender than the typical terrier, while the length suggests an Airedale.

Manchester Terrier

Bullbox Terrier

Any of the Bulldog breeds, which were originally developed to fight, or Mastiff breeds, which were bred to be fearsome guardians, could be part of this dog's heritage – especially as these dogs have been cross-bred since the late 1700s. Don't believe the fearsome reputation these dogs have; they're not hard to train and will be lively companions. They'll thrive in a home with teenagers who have similar high energy levels and enjoy playing with them. Such dogs are quite territorial by nature, though, and are alert to the presence of strangers. Training is important to keep their assertive side in check.

Staffordshire Bull Terrier

HEAD
Broad overall, with a short, wide muzzle and loose lips.

Bullmastiff

Staffordshire Bull Terrier

PAWS AND LEGS
Strong legs and big, powerful paws, like the Staffie's and Bulldog's. Well-muscled, curving thighs and straight front legs, like the Boxer's.

Boxer

Bulldog

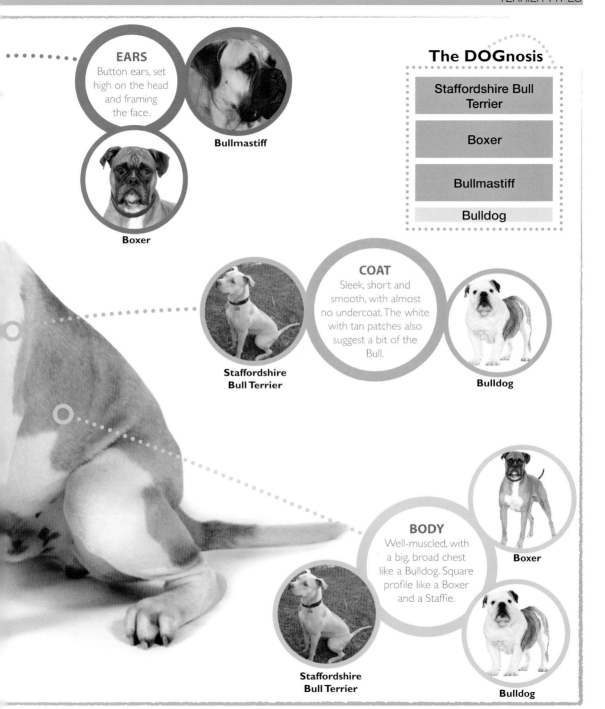

EARS
Button ears, set high on the head and framing the face.

Bullmastiff

Boxer

The DOGnosis

Staffordshire Bull Terrier
Boxer
Bullmastiff
Bulldog

COAT
Sleek, short and smooth, with almost no undercoat. The white with tan patches also suggest a bit of the Bull.

Staffordshire Bull Terrier

Bulldog

BODY
Well-muscled, with a big, broad chest like a Bulldog. Square profile like a Boxer and a Staffie.

Boxer

Staffordshire Bull Terrier

Bulldog

Lakelsh Foxder Terrier

This very unusual terrier was born without ears, which makes him one dog in a million ... or more! It has not affected his hearing, though. The absence of ears is the result of a genetic quirk. Although some breeds have much smaller ears than others, no external ear flaps at all is not a feature of any breed. With or without the ears, though, this dog is clearly a terrier. You can see it in his coat, his overall shape and even his grizzled little beard, not to mention his active and curious nature. This boy was born in Wales, so the Welsh Terrier is likely part of his ancestry. But you can see other influences, as well.

HEAD
Quite broad and short says Border Terrier, but he has a bit of a break between the forehead and the start of the muzzle, like both the Border and Fox Terriers.

Wire Fox Terrier

Border Terrier

Wire Fox Terrier

PAWS AND LEGS
The feet are round, compact and small like the Fox Terrier's, with relatively short thighs on the rear legs, like the Welsh Terrier's.

Welsh Terrier

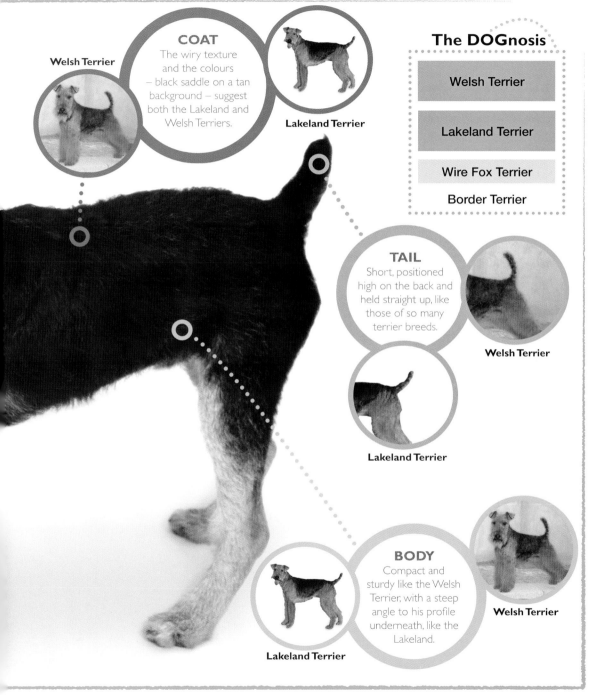

Welsh Terrier

COAT
The wiry texture and the colours – black saddle on a tan background – suggest both the Lakeland and Welsh Terriers.

Lakeland Terrier

The DOGnosis

Welsh Terrier
Lakeland Terrier
Wire Fox Terrier
Border Terrier

TAIL
Short, positioned high on the back and held straight up, like those of so many terrier breeds.

Welsh Terrier

Lakeland Terrier

BODY
Compact and sturdy like the Welsh Terrier, with a steep angle to his profile underneath, like the Lakeland.

Welsh Terrier

Lakeland Terrier

Irish Aire Terrier

One look at this dog and you know he's a terrier. It's the hard, wiry coat and beard on the muzzle that give it away. A rather tall terrier, in fact, which suggests an Airedale or Irish Terrier. But there's more to this boy, and his colouring suggests Lakeland or Welsh Terrier in his background, as well. He displays distinct terrier-like behaviour, too, which means he likes to explore and run and chase. He has plenty of energy, and those long legs help him move much faster than most terriers. He is bold by nature and will make a good guardian around the home.

HEAD

The ears are V-shaped and fold down away from the head, like all terrier breeds. The flat skull, the small break between the muzzle and the eyes and the dark, intense eyes, suggest Irish Terrier. The Lakeland's skull is also flat on top, with a strong muzzle.

Lakeland Terrier

Irish Terrier

Airedale Terrier

PAWS AND LEGS

Moderately long legs and strong hindquarters with no droop are from the Airedale, and the small, round feet with thick black nails are from the Welsh Terrier.

Welsh Terrier

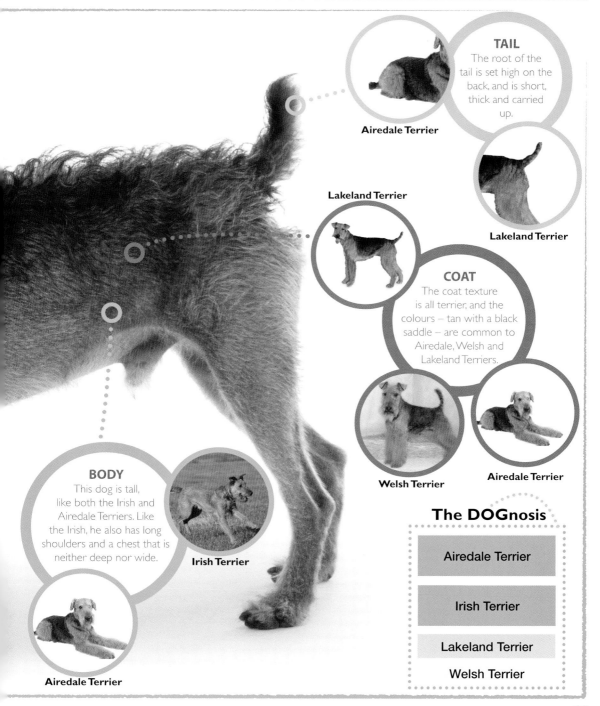

TAIL
The root of the tail is set high on the back, and is short, thick and carried up.

Airedale Terrier

Lakeland Terrier

Lakeland Terrier

COAT
The coat texture is all terrier, and the colours – tan with a black saddle – are common to Airedale, Welsh and Lakeland Terriers.

Welsh Terrier

Airedale Terrier

BODY
This dog is tall, like both the Irish and Airedale Terriers. Like the Irish, he also has long shoulders and a chest that is neither deep nor wide.

Irish Terrier

Airedale Terrier

The DOGnosis

Airedale Terrier
Irish Terrier
Lakeland Terrier
Welsh Terrier

Bullman Box Terrier

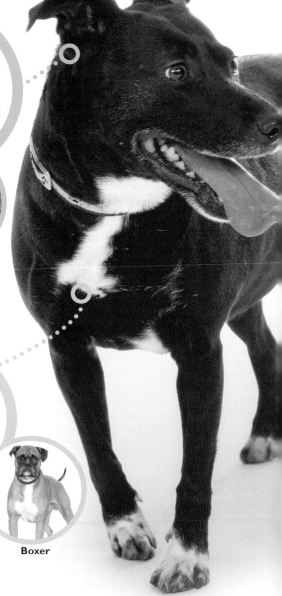

This dog's stocky appearance is due to her Bull Terrier genes, but a past cross with a Manchester Terrier might have been responsible for narrowing her face and extending the length of her muzzle. She is not very keen on running, with her body frame being better suited to ambling along. As a result, it is important to keep a check on her weight to ensure that she does not pile on the pounds. She's a loyal companion but can be rather short-tempered with other dogs, especially those who just run up to her. It's probably best to keep her on a leash in the park.

HEAD
The broad skull with a short muzzle suggests Staffordshire Bull Terrier, but the fact that the head is wedge-shaped and relatively long says Manchester Terrier.

Staffordshire Bull Terrier

Manchester Terrier

BODY
This stocky, compact, well-muscled body with a wide back and a broad, deep chest, is typical of the Staffie and the Boxer.

Staffordshire Bull Terrier

Boxer

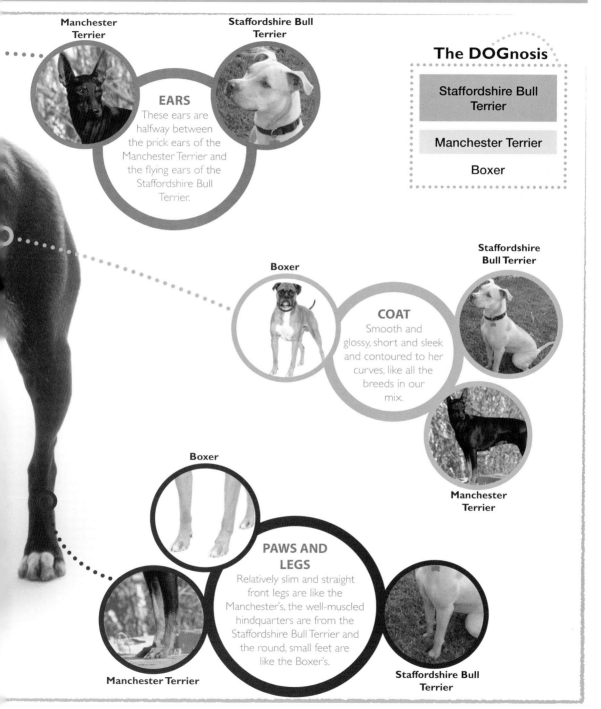

Manchester Terrier

Staffordshire Bull Terrier

EARS
These ears are halfway between the prick ears of the Manchester Terrier and the flying ears of the Staffordshire Bull Terrier.

The DOGnosis

| Staffordshire Bull Terrier |
| Manchester Terrier |
| Boxer |

Boxer

Staffordshire Bull Terrier

COAT
Smooth and glossy, short and sleek and contoured to her curves, like all the breeds in our mix.

Manchester Terrier

Boxer

PAWS AND LEGS
Relatively slim and straight front legs are like the Manchester's, the well-muscled hindquarters are from the Staffordshire Bull Terrier and the round, small feet are like the Boxer's.

Manchester Terrier

Staffordshire Bull Terrier

Miniature Vizdale

The beautiful colour and rough coat tell us this is a tall terrier with some hunting dog mixed in – perhaps the Vizsla. This is an energetic, exuberant dog with an inquisitive nature. Although some areas of his coat are longer than others, grooming is quite straightforward – just brush and go. Particular attention does need to be paid to the longer hair around his mouth, though. As with all terriers, the 'beard' can become soiled and matted by food. It's a good idea to wipe your terrier's face with a clean cloth every day after he eats. This is especially true if he eats wet food of any kind.

Border Terrier

HEAD
The head is strong and rectangular and flat on the top of the skull, like a Miniature Schnauzer's. The Border Terrier has a round muzzle with a distinctive break between the forehead and the muzzle.

Miniature Schnauzer

Airedale Terrier

PAWS AND LEGS
Straight, parallel front legs like the Schnauzer's and long, powerful thighs like the Airedale's.

Miniature Schnauzer

Border Terrier

COAT

That coat says Border Terrier: a short, dense undercoat with a wiry outercoat that lies close to body with no curls or waves. But the colour is Vizsla – solid golden rust.

Vizsla

The DOGnosis

Airedale Terrier
Vizsla
Border Terrier
Miniature Schnauzer

Airedale Terrier

TAIL

The Airedale's tail is carried up on the back; it is fairly long and thick. There is some feathering on the tail, like the Border Terrier's.

Border Terrier

Vizsla

BODY

The Vizsla contributes the gentle curve over the back, while the Schnauzer has a short, deep body with the ribs extending well down and the Border Terrier has a deep, narrow body with a tuck-up underneath.

Miniature Schnauzer

Border Terrier

Great Bullbox Terrier

Dogs of this type often used to be known as Bull and Terrier dogs. They're the other kind of terriers – the ones with the wide, blocky heads and short coats, rather than the wiry, scruffy sort. The brindle pattern comes from a working dog heritage, though. This is a powerfully built, energetic dog. He'll need to be well-trained to get all that energy under control. Working dogs need work to do; he is a dog who must have plenty of toys around to keep him occupied. He may also be wary around other dogs – training will help with that, too.

HEAD
The Staffordshire Bull Terrier has a broad skull and a medium length muzzle that's rounded on top. The Bullmastiff has a chiselled head with visible cheekbones, a broad, blunt muzzle, and lips that are loose but not pendulous.

Staffordshire Bull Terrier

Bullmastiff

Boxer

PAWS AND LEGS
The Staffordshire Bull Terrier's straight front legs and large bones combine here with the Boxer's broad, curved thighs.

Staffordshire Bull Terrier

Great Dane

EARS

This is a combination of the Staffordshire Bull Terrier's ears, which are set high and held out, and the Great Dane's ears, also high set, of medium thickness and size, and folded forwards.

Staffordshire Bull Terrier

The DOGnosis

| Staffordshire Bull Terrier |
| Boxer |
| Great Dane |
| Bullmastiff |

COAT

The coat is short, close, thick, glossy, and stiff, like those of all our breeds. The brindle and white could be Boxer, Bullmastiff or Great Dane.

Boxer

Bullmastiff

Staffordshire Bull Terrier

Great Dane

BODY

The look of overall strength and the muscular, slightly arched neck come from the Staffordshire Bull Terrier, while the Boxer brings a touch of lightness to the body, along with a deep chest and a moderate tuck-up at the tummy.

Boxer

Norpin Terrier

This little dog has the long body of the Norfolk and Australian Terriers and the longer legs of the Welsh Terrier, with the markings of the Miniature Pinscher (more commonly known as the Min Pin). Whatever the crosses, though, he displays all the typical terrier characteristics: lively, hardy, enthusiastic and bold by nature. In spite of his small size, he is no lap dog. He'll love being outside, whatever the weather. He'll become active and yappy if he's not given enough to do. And he's prone to chasing small animals. He'll also make you laugh with his energy and antics.

Norfolk Terrier

HEAD
The wide skull is slightly rounded on top and shaped like a wedge with a blunt end, like the Norfolk's. It's also long, like the Australian Terrier's, with the muzzle equalling the length of the skull.

Australian Terrier

Australian Terrier

BODY
The Australian and Norfolk Terriers have the longer back, while the Welsh Terrier's neck slopes gracefully into the shoulders, plus he has a level topline and good length of leg.

Norfolk Terrier

Welsh Terrier

Miniature Pinscher

EARS
Like the Min Pin's, the ears are large, V-shaped and set high on the skull. But Min Pin ears stand up. The Norfolk's button ears are the same shape but drop all the way over. This dog is halfway between the two.

Norfolk Terrier

The DOGnosis

Welsh Terrier
Australian Terrier
Miniature Pinscher

Norfolk Terrier

Miniature Pinscher

COAT
The Welsh Terrier has a hard, wiry coat that lies close to the body, with an undercoat. The Norfolk has a straight coat with a mane on the neck and shoulders. And the Min Pin is black with tan markings on the legs, chest and face.

Norfolk Terrier

Welsh Terrier

Norfolk Terrier

TAIL
Both the Australian and Norfolk Terriers have tails that are short and thick and are set high up on the rear. They hold their tails up or out.

Australian Terrier

Shepherd Dogs

Malabeau

This is a large, powerfully built, alert companion. It seems likely that the major influences in his ancestry were herding dogs, probably both the Beauceron and the Australian Shepherd, along with a dog from the far north – perhaps a Malamute or a Finnish Lapphund. And is there just a hint of Irish Terrier in those ears? This is a reserved dog – typical of the shepherds and the northern breeds – who will be loving and protective with his family but stand-offish with strangers. He needs plenty of exercise and must also be adequately trained because of his potentially dominant nature. His instincts may otherwise overwhelm him, causing him to misbehave as a result, with potentially serious consequences. But he is keen to learn and will form a very close bond with those in his immediate circle.

Irish Terrier

EARS
Set high and folded over the top of the skull.

Malamute

TAIL
Long and thick, like a Beauceron's, well furred and carried in a curl like those of the Nordic dogs.

Finnish Lapphund

Beauceron

PAWS AND LEGS
Powerful, well-muscled legs and large, rounded paws, suggestive of both the Beauceron and the Malamute.

Malamute

Beauceron

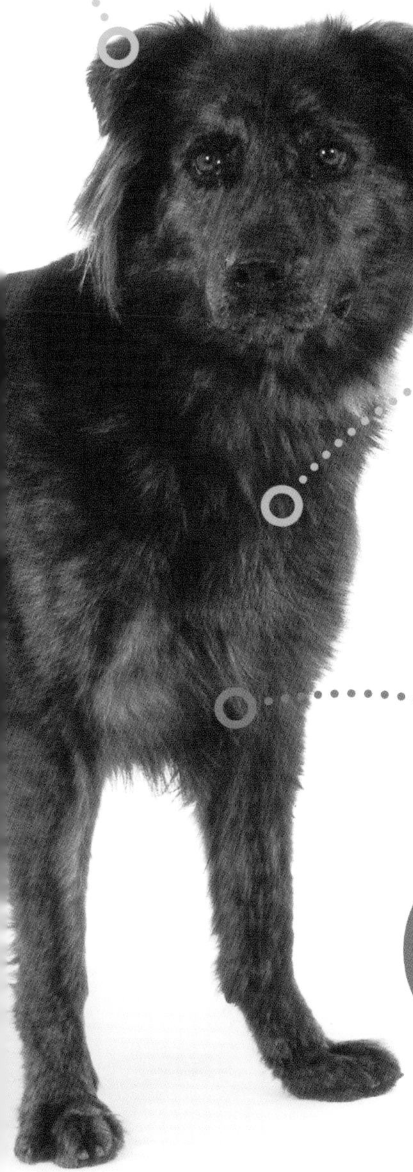

The DOGnosis

| Beauceron |
| Malamute/ Finnish Lapphund |
| Australian Shepherd |
| Irish Terrier |

Malamute

BODY
Broad chest and powerful build like the Beauceron and the northern breeds.

Finnish Lapphund

Beauceron

Finnish Lapphund

COAT
Medium length like the Australian Shepherd's; thicker on the sides of the face says Lapphund, but the overall colour is Beauceron black and tan.

Australian Shepherd

Beauceron

German Beagi

A quick look at this dog's head and you know at least one of his ancestors: the German Shepherd. It is quite unusual for one breed to be so dominant in a mutt's appearance. It's also interesting to see the head of such a tall dog on a body with such short legs. You might be thinking Basset Hound, but his legs are absolutely straight – which means it could be the Beagle's influence. There is even a white patch of fur on his chest, which supports this possibility. But that long, low body is not the Beagle type, either, so consider the Corgi. This dog is a lively character with plenty of energy, although he is likely not so responsive to training as a purebred German Shepherd might be (that hound independence from his Beagle blood).

German Shepherd

HEAD
Pure German Shepherd in every way.

TAIL
Long and held low, as a German Shepherd's, but bushy and a bit curved like the Corgi's.

Corgi

German Shepherd

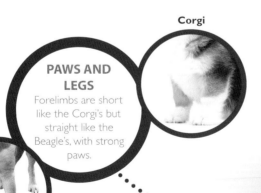

Corgi

PAWS AND LEGS
Forelimbs are short like the Corgi's but straight like the Beagle's, with strong paws.

Beagle

The DOGnosis

German Shepherd

Corgi

Beagle

German Shepherd

Corgi

BODY
Far longer than he is tall shows the Corgi influence, but the long, level back is German Shepherd.

COAT
Short, close-lying, and relatively coarse – that's Beagle – but the black saddle says German Shepherd.

German Shepherd

Beagle

Golden Belgian Collie

This dog seems to have a little bit of everything. The Belgian herder, the Malinois, is crossed in with a long-haired (rough) Collie, and the Golden Retriever ancestry shows up in her coat. There may even be a little sighthound blood lurking in her genes, as shown by her relatively long, slender legs and elongated neck. Her weather-resistant coat needs little grooming to maintain its attractive appearance. She has a very intelligent, responsive nature, being descended from breeds that have been developed over centuries to work closely alongside people. This is an active dog; she has a tendency to become restless at home and needs plenty of exercise and room to run. Confined indoors and left on her own for long periods, she'll soon become bored and, eventually, destructive.

Malinois

HEAD
The muzzle narrows slightly. The light, lean wedge of the head suggests a Collie, and the Malinois has powerful jaws.

Collie

Whippet

BODY
The Malinois is slightly longer than he is tall, with a powerful chest, while the tucked-up tummy suggests Whippet.

Malinois

PAWS AND LEGS
Strong and straight parallel forelegs, like those of a Malinois. A Collie may have provided the muscular thighs and padded feet.

Collie

Malinois

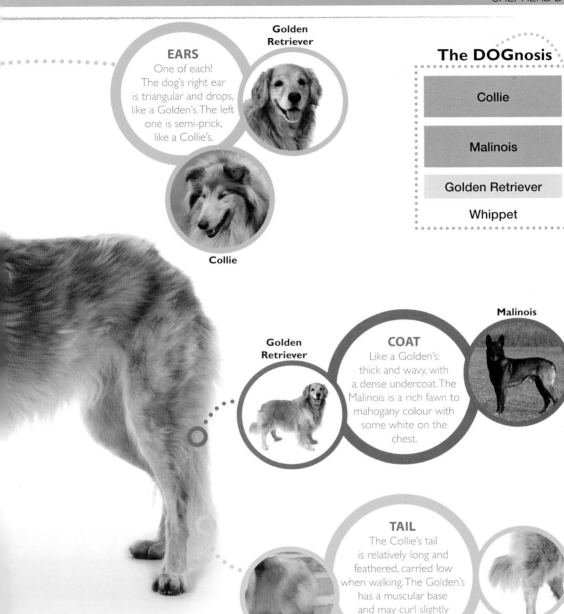

EARS
One of each!
The dog's right ear
is triangular and drops,
like a Golden's. The left
one is semi-prick,
like a Collie's.

Golden
Retriever

Collie

The DOGnosis

Collie
Malinois
Golden Retriever
Whippet

COAT
Like a Golden's:
thick and wavy, with
a dense undercoat. The
Malinois is a rich fawn to
mahogany colour with
some white on the
chest.

Golden
Retriever

Malinois

TAIL
The Collie's tail
is relatively long and
feathered, carried low
when walking. The Golden's
has a muscular base
and may curl slightly
upwards.

Collie

Golden
Retriever

Rhodesian Bullspitz

Fawn colouration with black around the muzzle is a combination that is not especially common in purebred dogs, but in this dog's case it gives us a clear clue as to his origins, especially when combined with the shape of his ears. These characteristics suggest that he is part Bullmastiff, crossed with a smaller, lighter breed – maybe the Finnish Spitz or the Norwegian Buhund. Bullmastiffs are intelligent and very loyal dogs, bred as gamekeeper's companions in the 1800s. His narrower face, along with his coat texture and body type, suggest the influence of the Rhodesian Ridgeback, perhaps with a little Labrador Retriever tossed in. This dog is a smart, loyal companion, anxious to learn and will readily alert you to the approach of strangers.

Labrador Retriever

Bullmastiff

EARS
V-shaped drop ears are set high and back on the head.

Norwegian Buhund

COAT
The short, sleek coat is a Bullmastiff's, but a lighter chest and the black around the muzzle says Buhund.

Bullmastiff

Labrador Retriever

TAIL
Thick and powerful like a Lab's, set low like a Bullmastiff's.

Bullmastiff

Rhodesian Ridgeback

HEAD

Reasonably short but tapering muzzle and broad head, suggestive of the Ridgeback and the northern breeds.

The DOGnosis

Bullmastiff
Rhodesian Ridgeback
Labrador Retriever

Finnish Spitz/
Norwegian Buhund

Norwegian Buhund

Finnish Spitz

Bullmastiff

BODY

His muscular body, with a broad back and a barrel chest, is characteristic of all of these breeds.

Labrador Retriever

Rhodesian Ridgeback

Wegieman Boxhound

A very clear shepherd dog influence is apparent in the appearance of this dog's muzzle and ears. He looks a bit like a German Shepherd or a Norwegian Elkhound (which one figures into the mix depends on where you live), but has a relatively short coat and a lighter build. His overall makeup suggests one of the Belgian herding breeds, as well – possibly the Malinois. However, his brindle colouration is very distinctive and is not seen in the shepherd breeds. Among the breeds where you do see it is the Boxer, which his body type also resembles. The result lightened his frame and gave him a straighter back, without compromising his stamina. This dog has an athletic nature and plenty of energy, which means he needs a home with a big garden, as well as plenty of opportunity to exercise farther afield.

Malinois

Boxer

BODY
Athletic, with a relatively straight back, suggesting both a Boxer and a Malinois.

German Shepherd

TAIL
Carried quite low, with longer hair than on the body.

Malinois

COAT
Short and sleek like that of a Malinois, with a brindle pattern, as is sometimes found on Boxers.

Malinois

Boxer

German
Shepherd

HEAD
Strong and slender,
with a tapering
muzzle that is about
half the length of the
head.

Norwegian
Elkhound

Malinois

EARS
Broad at the base,
prick and set a little
wide – traits of both
the German Shepherd
and the Elkhound.

Norwegian
Elkhound

German
Shepherd

The DOGnosis

German Shepherd
Norwegian Elkhound
Boxer
Malinois

Petibeard Bor-Collie

Bearded Collie

You may be wondering how such a scruffy looking dog ended up with the shepherds, but the fact is that there are some scruffy herding dogs. This girl looks most like a Bearded Collie, a breed developed to herd sheep in the border lands of England and Scotland. A key difference is that her coat is much shorter and scruffier, though. One of the rough-coated French scenthounds (dogs who follow prey by scent), such as the Petit Basset Griffon Vendeen (known fondly, and more simply, as the PBGV), may be in the mix here. She'll need a quick brushing almost every day to keep away the tangles. This is very much an active dog (some Border Collie blood will reinforce that) who needs lots of exercise and a job to do – even if it's just playing with the kids.

HEAD
The broad skull and square muzzle suggest both a Bearded Collie and a PBGV.

Petit Basset Griffon Vendeen

Border Collie

COAT
That long, wiry outer coat with an insulating undercoat is typical of the Beardie and the PBGV, but the black and white looks more like a Border Collie.

Petit Basset Griffon Vendeen

Bearded Collie

EARS
Set quite far back on the head and hanging down, like those of a PBGV or a Bearded Collie.

Petit Basset Griffon Vendeen

Bearded Collie

Border Collie

BODY
Medium size, just a bit longer than the dog is tall, with a rounded rib cage – traits shared by the Border Collie and the PBGV.

Petit Basset Griffon Vendeen

PAWS AND LEGS
Shorter hair on the legs and paws is more Border Collie, while the large feet say PBGV.

Border Collie

Petit Basset Griffon Vendeen

Golden Butervita

Mutts can sometimes be very elegant, as this dog demonstrates. Her stunning golden-red, plush coat, beautiful head and bright, round eyes are a very attractive combination. Her Nordic background is evident in her curled tail, reddish colour and the lovely shape of her head. Then add in a little herding dog, in the form of a Tervuren, and a coat texture like that of the Golden Retriever. The Golden shows up in her disposition, too. She is a responsive companion, easy to train and eager to please. This is a dog who just wants a job to do for you.

HEAD
Long, elegant head with a pointed muzzle and round, bright eyes.

Tervuren

Norwegian Buhund

TAIL
Well-furred and held low with a gentle curve, like a Golden's or a Tervuren's.

Golden Retriever

Golden Retriever

Tervuren

Golden Retriever

COAT
The relatively long, straight hair and golden colour is Golden Retriever, but the deeper red comes from the Buhund. The heavier feathering on the neck, chest and tail says Tervuren.

Tervuren

Norwegian Buhund

Akita

Norwegian Buhund

EARS
Prick ears set wide on the head and well-furred at the base.

Tervuren

Akita

Golden Retriever

BODY
Long, broad, level back and a strong body overall, suggestive of both an Akita and a Golden.

The DOGnosis

Akita

Golden Retriever

Norwegian Buhund

Tervuren

Boxshep Bullsla

This dog is determined and self-assured – a reflection of her likely ancestry of German Shepherd and Staffordshire Bull Terrier. She is a loyal companion and will prove to be a fearless guardian, but she will need to be properly trained to prevent her from becoming testy with other dogs. Not that she's all serious-minded; she also has a very playful side to her nature, inherited from her Boxer blood. And her Vizsla side (the heritage of Hungarian hunting dogs) only adds to her trainability and her high activity level.

Staffordshire Bull Terrier

Boxer

EARS
Triangular ears are set high in the head like a Staffie's and fold forward like a Boxer's.

German Shepherd

COAT
Relatively short and glossy, with a reddish hue, like a Vizsla's, but longer, like a German Shepherd's.

Vizsla

PAWS AND LEGS
The hind legs extend out behind the body, like a German Shepherd's, while the broad and curved thighs are like a Boxer's.

Boxer

German Shepherd

German Shepherd

HEAD
The square skull, broad and flat on top, with strong jaws, is from a Staffie. The wedge shape with a tapering muzzle suggests German Shepherd, but those chiselled cheeks are Vizsla.

Vizsla

Staffordshire Bull Terrier

German Shepherd

Staffordshire Bull Terrier

BODY
Powerful, with a curve to the topline, a muscular physique, and a broad back: it all says German Shepherd and Staffie.

The DOGnosis

Boxer
German Shepherd
Staffordshire Bull Terrier
Vizsla

Collinois Shepherd

Here is a dog who looks very much like a scaled-down German Shepherd, but his overall lightness suggests there may also be some Collie in him, too (specifically, the short-haired, or smooth Collie). The influence of both these herding breeds is also evident in the very positive way he responds to training. He is very energetic and playful by nature, and is ideal for a home with older children, particularly if there is a garden or backyard where they can run around together. He also needs to be taken out for walks in an area where he can be exercised safely off the leash.

HEAD
The German Shepherd's head is cleanly chiselled, and the skull slopes into a long muzzle that is somewhat blunt at the end. But this head is a bit narrower than a typical German Shepherd's — more like that of a Malinois.

German Shepherd

Malinois

COAT
The colouration — black saddle and facial markings, tan on the rest — is German Shepherd. But the splashes of white on the feet and chest are Collie colours. And the very intense black on the saddle is Doberman.

German Shepherd

Doberman Pinscher

German Shepherd

Collie

Malinois

TAIL
On both the German Shepherd and the Malinois, the tail is long, thick, well-feathered, hangs in a slight curve and is carried low, except when the dog is excited.

The DOGnosis

German Shepherd
Collie
Malinois

Doberman Pinscher

EARS

These are purely
Collie ears: set wide
on the head, triangular,
and about three-
quarters erect.

Collie

Collie

BODY

The round and
moderately long muscular
neck, and the fact that the top
of the shoulders is slightly higher
than the rump, suggests a German
Shepherd, as does the level back
and gently rounded loin. But this
dog's body is a bit lighter overall
– more like a Doberman's
or a Collie's.

**Doberman
Pinscher**

**German
Shepherd**

Swiss Border Collab

It's rare to see a dog whose facial markings are split right down the middle; it's a striking feature here. His colouration suggests one of the Swiss Mountain Dogs, most likely the Greater Swiss because that's the one with short hair. Speaking of short hair, both the Collie and the Border Collie can have long hair or short. This dog clearly takes after the short-haired varieties. His mixed ancestry has resulted in a well-balanced, friendly mutt who thrives on attention and will adapt well to family life. Here is a dog who will happily spend hours playing with the kids.

Greater Swiss Mountain Dog

Labrador Retriever

HEAD
The skull is wide between the ears, the cheeks are well-defined and the flews (the lips) are tight but extend just below the jaw. Both the Lab and the Greater Swiss Mountain Dog have these traits.

Collie

COAT
The texture of the coat suggests the Collies. Both have a double coat with a weather-resistant, straight, flat outercoat and a dense undercoat. The colouration is Swissie: black, white and tan, with black on the upper part of the body and the ears.

Greater Swiss Mountain Dog

Border Collie

Border Collie

TAIL
The long, thick tail is carried down, except when the dog is excited, and is more thickly furred at the end.

Greater Swiss Mountain Dog

Border Collie

EARS

The Collie has V-shaped ears that taper to a point and naturally fold over up high near the tip. On the Border Collie, the ears can be up, down or in-between.

Collie

Border Collie

Collie

BODY

The Border Collie is broad-chested with good lung capacity and the Collie is rectangular (just a bit longer than tall), as is the Greater Swiss Mountain Dog, who is quite long in the leg and has a level back.

Greater Swiss Mountain Dog

The DOGnosis

Greater Swiss Mountain Dog
Border Collie
Collie
Labrador Retriever

Border Collita

Two types of Collies and the largest dog in Japan – the Akita – have contributed to this dog's ancestry. What else is in the mix is a difficult mystery to unravel. But the input of these breeds has resulted in a thick coat that will require a fair amount of grooming. He also has a wary nature, particularly when it comes to strangers, but is a loyal companion with those he knows well. Akitas have a tendency to be aggressive with other dogs, but the gentler Collie nature should help balance that trait.

EARS
The Border Collie can have ears that are up or ears that are down. If they are drop ears, they should not be too large or hang like a scenthound's ears.

Border Collie

BODY
Big, firmly muscled, with a wide, deep chest and level back, suggestive of an Akita. Like a Border Collie, he is athletic and a bit longer than tall, supported by powerful hips and thighs.

Border Collie

Akita

Akita

TAIL
The Akita has a large and full tail, set high and carried up and curled, with full, straight, coarse hair. The Collie has a well-furred tail with an upward swirl at the tip.

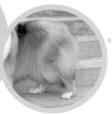

Collie

The DOGnosis

Collie
Akita
Border Collie

HEAD

This head has the refinement of a Collie's — a lean wedge that tapers cleanly to the tip of the well-rounded muzzle. But there's also something a bit broader and flatter about it, and that's the Border Collie influence.

Border Collie

Collie

Collie

COAT

This is the Akita's double coat with a thick undercoat and a straight, harsh outercoat that stands off the body. But there's a little too much brown and black for an Akita — the colouration is more like a Collie's.

Akita

Tervman Rottamute

The influence of some of the larger working breeds can clearly be seen in this dog – her head suggests Rottweiler and the density of her coat means perhaps a Malamute (bred in Alaska), but there is definitely some shepherd in the mix as well. Her size means she will need a lot of space and plenty of off-leash exercise. She has an active nature and wants to be trained and kept busy. She is also an alert guardian. Dogs of this type tend to be good with children, especially teenagers. They may be too powerful for younger children, although their large size enables them to withstand rough-and-tumble play.

Rottweiler

HEAD
The Rottweiler's head is of medium length, broad between the ears and powerful, with a well-muscled neck. The Malamute's is moderately rounded between the ears with a large, bulky muzzle.

Malamute

COAT
The Tervuren's coat is long, straight and dense, and the Malamute's is medium-long and very thick. The pattern is a German Shepherd's – tan with a black saddle and black markings on the head.

Malamute

Tervuren

Tervuren

German Shepherd

PAWS AND LEGS
Strong, straight, parallel legs are like the Rottweiler's and Tervuren's. The large, compact feet are from the Malamute.

Rottweiler

Malamute

**German
Shepherd**

EARS
These ears are a cross between the German Shepherd's large V-shaped prick ears, which are set on the sides of the head, and the Rottweiler's drop ears, which are also wide-set but hang down and forward.

Rottweiler

**German
Shepherd**

BODY
The broad, deep, roomy chest is like a Rottweiler's, while the straight back and the fact that the dog is longer than she is tall suggests a German Shepherd.

Rottweiler

The DOGnosis

German Shepherd
Rottweiler
Malamute
Tervuren

Hound Types

Ibizan Whiphound

Whippet

This dog is clearly of sighthound stock – bred to chase down game by following it visually rather than with his nose. His sleek body, head shape and sloping back are all clues to his ancestry. He looks as if he is partly Whippet, although his very distinctive prick ears (sometimes called 'candle flame') suggest that the Ibizan Hound or a similar breed has also played a part in his past. A friendly companion to those in their immediate circle, sighthounds have a healthy suspicion of strangers and may seem aloof to those they do not know well. They also love to chase anything that moves. It is very easy to maintain his sleek appearance – a grooming glove is all you'll need. His exercise needs are quite modest, in spite of his athletic build, as he is suited to sprinting rather than long-distance running. In cold or wet weather, however, he is likely to need a coat.

HEAD
Slender and elegant like all sighthounds. The large, dark eyes suggest Whippet. The long, smooth muzzle with a slight Roman bump is from the Ibizan Hound.

Ibizan Hound

PAWS AND LEGS
Slender and strong like the Whippet's, there's not much curve in the rear legs. Like the Manchester Terrier, he has straight forelegs, muscular thighs and compact feet.

Whippet

Manchester Terrier

EARS
You've got to love those ears! They're large, pointed and always up.

Ibizan Hound

The DOGnosis

Whippet
Ibizan Hound
Manchester Terrier

Whippet

COAT
This dog's colour and pattern are all his own – a sign of his gloriously mixed heritage. Like the Whippet's coat, it lies smooth and close to the body, and like the Ibizan's, it's short and hard.

Ibizan Hound

BODY
The back has a graceful, natural arch over the loin, and the bottom of the chest reaches almost to the elbows, as on a Whippet. The Manchester Terrier has a slightly arched, elegant yet strong neck.

Whippet

Manchester Terrier

Grey Ibizan Slippet

This elegant girl is clearly of Greyhound descent, but her frame is slightly stockier than a purebred Greyhound and her head is not as narrow. Her typical sighthound profile represents one of the earliest forms of the domestic dog. Since humans started developing breeds, Greyhounds have figured into many dogs – added to various mixes to give each particular new breed speed and light-ness. This dog's colouring suggests that perhaps one of the Mediterranean hounds, such as the Ibizan Hound, may have played a part in her ancestry. And her head and ears suggest a little Whippet mixed with Saluki. All these sighthounds are active, independent and love to run. Taking them off the leash in an unfenced area is always a risk, because if they see some-thing moving out of the corner of their eye, they're off!

Greyhound

BODY
The long, level back suggests the Ibizan connection, while the deep chest and tucked-up tummy are from the Greyhound.

Ibizan Hound

TAIL
Long and held quite low, tapering, with a slight upward curve.

Ibizan Hound

Whippet

Greyhound

PAWS AND LEGS
Straight front legs and well-muscled hindquarters say Saluki. The strong wrists and ankles and tight feet are Whippet traits.

Saluki

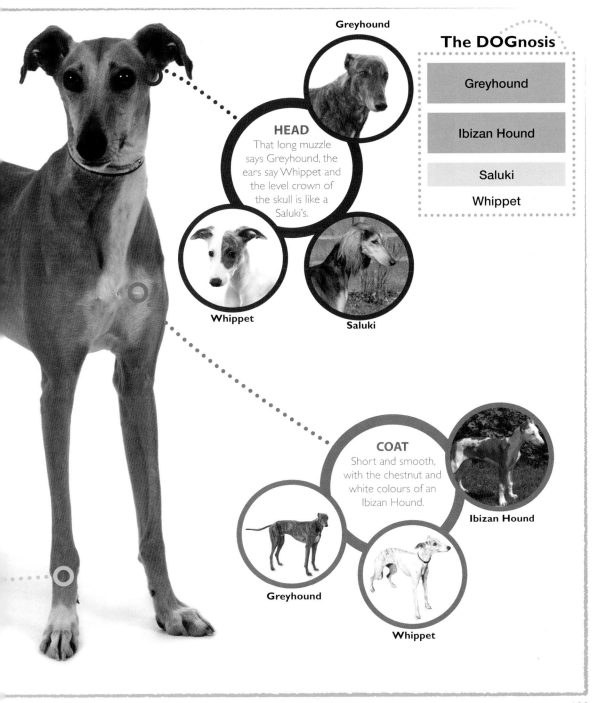

Greyhound

HEAD
That long muzzle says Greyhound, the ears say Whippet and the level crown of the skull is like a Saluki's.

Whippet

Saluki

The DOGnosis

Greyhound

Ibizan Hound

Saluki

Whippet

COAT
Short and smooth, with the chestnut and white colours of an Ibizan Hound.

Ibizan Hound

Greyhound

Whippet

Scodeeret Hound

The relatively coarse texture of this dog's coat is described as 'wirehaired'. This characteristic is seen in many of the terriers and a few other breeds, and helps to protect them from injury when running through underbrush. This boy's tousled appearance is augmented by a beard of longer hair on the chin. He is also a large dog, and so could have Scottish Deerhound or Irish Wolfhound blood in his ancestry – or even both. Certainly, he is powerfully built and able to run. The shape of his tail and his relatively broad head also hint at a hunting dog ancestry, maybe one of the German Pointers. It seems quite possible that there may be a Labrador Retriever lurking in his past, too. He certainly has an enthusiastic nature and loves the outdoor life.

Scottish Deerhound

HEAD
He has the strong jaws of a Lab, the square, bearded muzzle of a Scottish Deerhound and the angular head of a German Shorthaired Pointer.

Labrador Retriever

German Shorthaired Pointer

PAWS AND LEGS
Broad forelegs with long front paws and long, powerful legs front and back, say hound and more hound.

Scottish Deerhound

Irish Wolfhound

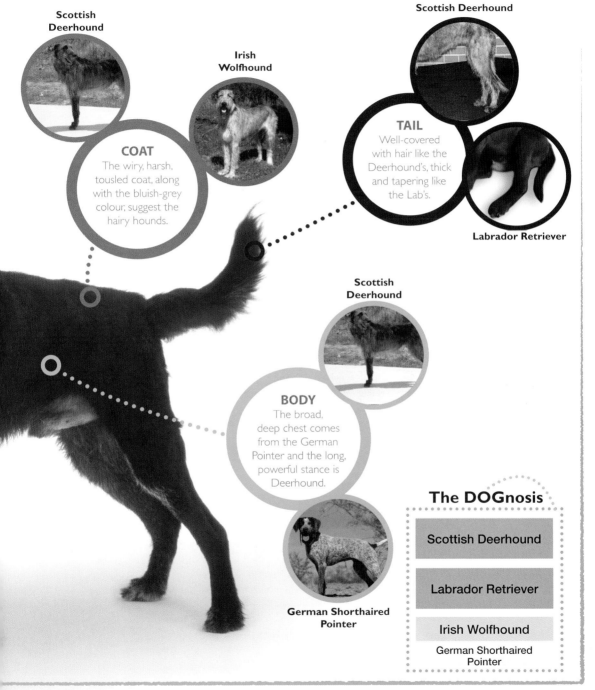

Scottish Deerhound

Irish Wolfhound

Scottish Deerhound

COAT
The wiry, harsh, tousled coat, along with the bluish-grey colour, suggest the hairy hounds.

TAIL
Well-covered with hair like the Deerhound's, thick and tapering like the Lab's.

Labrador Retriever

Scottish Deerhound

BODY
The broad, deep chest comes from the German Pointer and the long, powerful stance is Deerhound.

German Shorthaired Pointer

The DOGnosis

Scottish Deerhound

Labrador Retriever

Irish Wolfhound

German Shorthaired Pointer

Basset Corgle

It might be easiest to say this dog has the head of a Corgi, the body of a Basset Hound and the eyes and tail of a Beagle. But of course, nothing is that easy in the world of mutts. How could three dogs mate to produce this little boy? Like every mutt, his mixture is something of a mystery, but we can see some clear characteristics that at least tell us he's part scenthound (dogs who track their prey by following a scent trail) with a little shepherd thrown in. This is borne out by his temperament; he's enthusiastic by nature (shepherd), but rather stubborn as well (scenthound). Training will not be easy, although perseverance will pay off. It's important to keep him well-exercised, so he does not become fat.

Corgi

HEAD
Flat cheeks, with a strong, pointed muzzle suggest the Corgi, but the relatively long skull with large eyes is Beagle.

Beagle

Basset Hound

PAWS AND LEGS
Short legs with rounded paws are like a Corgi's, but the legs are not entirely straight and the paws are large and point outwards, like a Basset Hound's.

Corgi

EARS
Large, triangular, tulip ears are rounded at the tips.

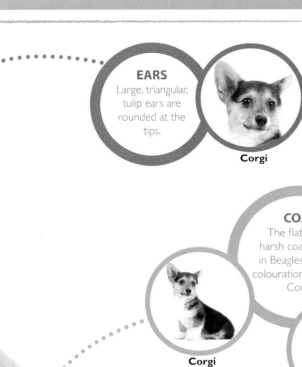

Corgi

Corgi

Basset Hound

Beagle

COAT
The flat, lightly harsh coat is seen in Beagles, but the colouration is from a Corgi.

Corgi

Beagle

Basset Hound

BODY
Deep-bodied and short-legged says Corgi, and that paunch around the middle shows a bit of the Basset.

Corgi

Border Clippet

This dog's head, coat and colour all say Border Collie. But she's taller and more slender than a typical Border Collie, and that's a clue that a sighthound, such as a Whippet, lurks somewhere in the mix. While Border Collies can have short hair, long hair or something in-between, this dog's coat suggests a little spaniel. Perhaps a Brittany – they're most commonly red and white, but they come in black and white, too. So what we have here is a mix of herding dog, hunting dog and sighthound. She definitely likes to run. Taking off her leash anywhere outdoors is going to be an adventure.

HEAD
Slightly domed skull, with a medium-length, tapering muzzle and bright, intense eyes. One look at a Border Collie says it all.

Border Collie

PAWS AND LEGS
Straight, slender forelegs and strong thighs are Whippet traits, while the round feet and well-arched toes are from the Collie.

Collie

Whippet

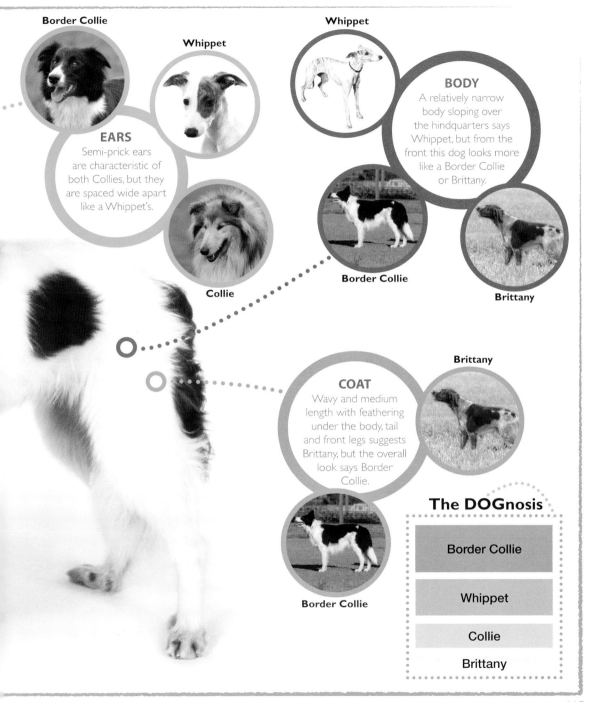

Border Collie

Whippet

EARS
Semi-prick ears are characteristic of both Collies, but they are spaced wide apart like a Whippet's.

Whippet

BODY
A relatively narrow body sloping over the hindquarters says Whippet, but from the front this dog looks more like a Border Collie or Brittany.

Collie

Border Collie

Brittany

Brittany

COAT
Wavy and medium length with feathering under the body, tail and front legs suggests Brittany, but the overall look says Border Collie.

Border Collie

The DOGnosis

| Border Collie |
| Whippet |
| Collie |
| Brittany |

115

Ibish Terhound

This dog seems to be a cross between a hound and a terrier. She's tall and slim, like a fast sighthound, but that wiry coat always makes us think of a terrier – until we remember that a few hounds also have that type of coat. The Irish Wolfhound comes to mind. And, oddly, because of those big ears, the Ibizan Hound does too. They are rare, but Ibizans do occasionally show up with a wire coat. Of course, the explanation could also be a lot simpler: a tall, red terrier, such as the Irish Terrier, could be in this dog's background. She will not do well in the city because she needs plenty of opportunities to explore and exercise. Her terrier-hound heritage may also make her wary of strangers.

Irish Wolfhound

HEAD
The long skull, with a long and moderately pointed muzzle, looks like a Wolfhound's, while the dark brown, intense eyes are like an Irish Terrier's.

Irish Terrier

BODY
The long back is characteristic of both Irish breeds. The tucked-up belly is a Wolfhound trait and the slight curve of the topline looks Ibizan.

Irish Terrier

Irish Wolfhound

Ibizan Hound

EARS

Those large prick ears are all Ibizan Hound.

Ibizan Hound

The DOGnosis

Irish Wolfhound
Irish Terrier
Ibizan Hound

Irish Wolfhound

COAT

Dense and wiry, lying close to the body, not kinky or curly and a rich red – all suggestive of an Irish Terrier. Red is also a possibility for the Wolfhound, whose coat is rough and hard, and especially wiry and long over the eyes and under the jaw.

Irish Terrier

Irish Wolfhound

TAIL

The tail is slightly curved and well-covered with hair like a Wolfhound's, but the curve and the fact that it is set low on the back says Ibizan Hound.

Ibizan Hound

Foxagle Rhodehound

This dog is all hunting hound. Alert and powerfully built, he is a strong, almost effortless runner, thanks partly to his long legs. His hound heritage gives him good stamina, too – his ancestors followed quarry over large areas, hunting mostly by scent. He'll need plenty of exercise every day and must be allowed to run off the leash. Although he has strong hunting instincts, thanks to his origins, he is otherwise a very gentle dog by nature and makes an excellent companion. He cannot be entirely trusted with very small dogs, cats or similar small pets, though.

Rhodesian Ridgeback

HEAD
The Foxhound's head is full but not heavy, with a clean neck and a straight, blunt muzzle. Like the Ridgeback, he has well-chiselled cheeks and his ears are set very high on his head.

Foxhound

COAT
The coat is short, dense, hard and glossy, like a Foxhound's. The Beagle colouring is evident in the tan and black with the splash of white on the chest and muzzle.

Beagle

Foxhound

TAIL
Both the Foxhound and the Beagle have a tail set moderately high, which is carried up and has a slight brush at the end.

Beagle

Foxhound

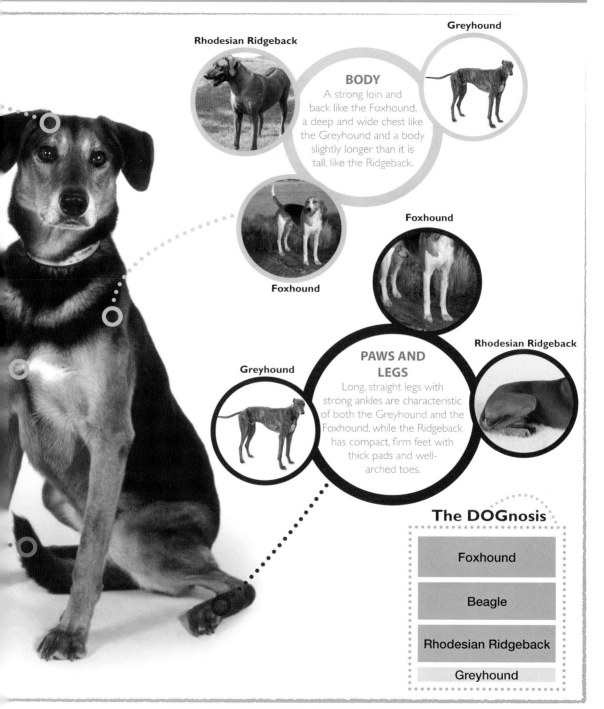

Rhodesian Ridgeback

Greyhound

BODY
A strong loin and back like the Foxhound, a deep and wide chest like the Greyhound and a body slightly longer than it is tall, like the Ridgeback.

Foxhound

Foxhound

PAWS AND LEGS
Long, straight legs with strong ankles are characteristic of both the Greyhound and the Foxhound, while the Ridgeback has compact, firm feet with thick pads and well-arched toes.

Greyhound

Rhodesian Ridgeback

The DOGnosis

Foxhound
Beagle
Rhodesian Ridgeback
Greyhound

Scottish Grey Zoiluki

Scottish Deerhound

This dog's long legs, powerful hindquarters, long whip tail and tucked-up tummy tell you he's a sighthound. He also has a deep chest and good lung capacity, which means he has enough oxygen to accelerate very quickly. This dog is a sprinter, and you will have to be careful with him when he is not on a leash. His size, coat and head shape make it pretty clear that there is some Greyhound and Scottish Deerhound in his background. Perhaps there may also be some exotic blood from the very elegant Borzoi of Russia and Saluki of Persia.

HEAD
Broad at the ears, with a pointed muzzle that tapers to the nose, suggests Deerhound. Like the Borzoi's, the muzzle is level on top and the nose is large and black.

Borzoi

COAT
The Deerhound's coat is harsh, wiry, long, thick, close-lying and ragged. The Saluki contributes an overall softer, silkier texture and feathering on the legs, shoulders and ears.

Saluki

Scottish Deerhound

Saluki

PAWS AND LEGS
The long, broad, straight forelegs and powerful hindquarters are Deerhound traits. The Saluki contributes feet of moderate length that are not overly compact and are well-arched.

Scottish Deerhound

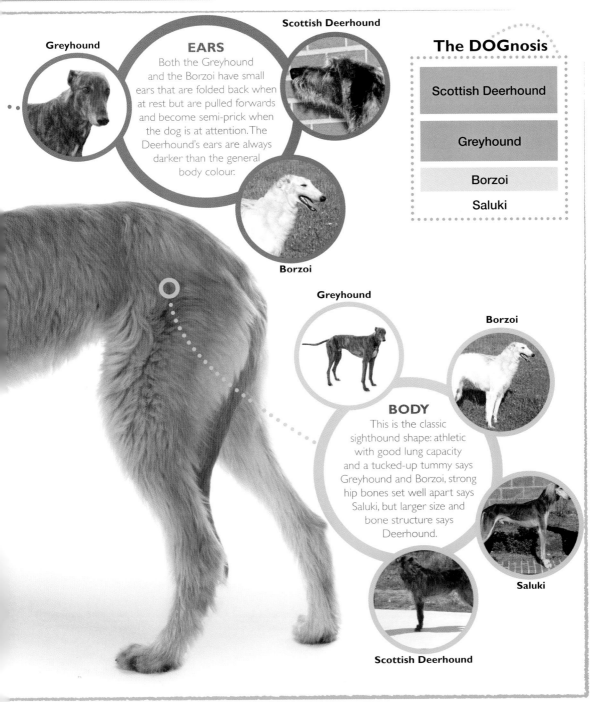

Greyhound

Scottish Deerhound

EARS
Both the Greyhound and the Borzoi have small ears that are folded back when at rest but are pulled forwards and become semi-prick when the dog is at attention. The Deerhound's ears are always darker than the general body colour.

Borzoi

The DOGnosis

Scottish Deerhound

Greyhound

Borzoi

Saluki

Greyhound

Borzoi

BODY
This is the classic sighthound shape: athletic with good lung capacity and a tucked-up tummy says Greyhound and Borzoi, strong hip bones set well apart says Saluki, but larger size and bone structure says Deerhound.

Saluki

Scottish Deerhound

121

Foxy Whipspring

Whippet

Looking at this dog's colouration, long legs and body profile, a scenthound, such as a Foxhound (or a Hamiltonstovare, if you live in Scandinavia), comes to mind. Yet his muzzle is longer and his ears are smaller and are set farther back on his head. A look at the Smooth Fox Terrier accounts for some of these differences. A bit of sighthound is evident in his elegant body, too. He's got plenty of stamina when he's exercising, and is going to be an active dog with a mind of his own. He will need training that takes into account the fact that he is easily distracted by interesting scents and moving objects.

HEAD
The skull is long and flat on top, with not much of a break between the forehead and the muzzle, and strong jaws, like the Fox Terrier's. Wide between the ears and tapering to the nose are Whippet traits.

Smooth Fox Terrier

PAWS AND LEGS
The Foxhound and the Hamiltonstovare have strong, perfectly straight front legs, especially at the ankles, and the feet are round and catlike. Like the Whippet's, this dog's legs are long in proportion to his body.

Whippet

Hamiltonstovare

Foxhound

Smooth Fox Terrier

Foxhound

EARS

The Fox Terrier has small, V-shaped, button ears that are set high on the head, like this dog's, but the terrier's ears fall forwards. These ears fall more to the side, like those of the scenthounds.

The DOGnosis

Foxhound/
Hamiltonstovare

Smooth Fox Terrier

Whippet

English Springer Spaniel

COAT

The tricolour pattern is typical scenthound, as is the short, hard, dense, glossy coat. But the speckling on the legs suggests the English Springer Spaniel.

Hamiltonstovare

English Springer Spaniel

Hamiltonstovare

BODY

The absolutely level topline and relatively straight thighs indicate the scenthounds, but the slender build and tucked-up tummy are Whippet traits.

Foxhound

Whippet

Great Grey Pointing Hound

A lively, athletic nature suggests this dog is descended from a combination of hound and working stock. He looks a bit like a Greyhound in build, but with a different head. Other large breeds are in his ancestry as well, probably including a Great Dane. The one-of-each ears illustrate how random genetics can be in mutts. It's also the case that the ears of young dogs sometimes fold over at first and later stand up. Training is important for this dog, just because he's so large. If he bounds up to people, full of exuberance, he could easily knock someone over.

Pointer

HEAD
Like the Pointer's, the skull is as wide as the muzzle is long. The muzzle is deep and strong, and the flews (lips) don't hang loosely. Like the Greyhound's, the skull is long and wide between the ears. The eyes are round and are set wide apart.

Greyhound

PAWS AND LEGS
Long, slender, but strong legs like the Greyhound's, oval feet with tight, arched toes like the Pointer's and the elbows set half the distance from the top of the shoulder to the ground, like the Great Dane's.

Greyhound

Great Dane

Pointer

Greyhound

COAT
This coat is short, thick, clean and glossy. Greyhounds and Great Danes come in many colours and patterns, including brindle – even with the white splashes.

Great Dane

The DOGnosis

Greyhound
Great Dane
Pointer

BODY
Like the Great Dane, this dog has a long, powerful body, a level back, a wide chest and a well-arched, strong neck. Like the Greyhound, he's tall and lithe but strong, with a tucked-up tummy.

Greyhound

Great Dane

Pointer

TAIL
The tail is thick at the base, tapering and medium-long, like a Great Dane's. The Pointer's tail is also heavier at the root and is not carried between the legs.

Great Dane

Grey Zippet Hound

Who is this masked hound? She is certainly a sighthound – a dog who tracks prey by sight rather than scent. These dogs were once used to hunt both small and large animals, such as stags, wolves and hares, and they needed to be fast and large. Sighthounds are sprinters, and they should, ideally, be exercised in an open area where they can run unimpeded, rather than in than in woodland, where they can never quite get up to speed. When she's off the leash, keep this dog away from roads and small dogs. Quiet and affectionate by nature, the big sighthounds make good family pets, although they are usually quite reserved with strangers.

HEAD
The Whippet's skull is long and lean, fairly wide between the ears, and tapers to a long, powerful muzzle. The large nose is a Borzoi trait.

Borzoi

Whippet

BODY
The Borzoi has a strong, level back, a deep chest and a pronounced tuck-up in the tummy. The Greyhound has a long, strong, elegantly arched neck. Both are large, tall dogs.

Borzoi

Greyhound

EARS

The ears are all Ibizan Hound: large, erect and set on the corners of the skull, with rounded tips.

Ibizan Hound

Greyhound

The DOGnosis

Greyhound
Borzoi
Whippet

Ibizan Hound

COAT

The smooth, short coat contours the body, as on Greyhounds and Whippets. The tan colour is typical of a Greyhound, while that mask may be the Borzoi connection.

Whippet

Borzoi

Borzoi

TAIL

The moderately long tail tapers to a point and is held down low near the legs, like the Ibizan Hound's. It is carried in a graceful curve, like the Borzoi's.

Ibizan Hound

Greyscot Waterpoo

This his dog is built for speed. There's a strong Greyhound influence evident in his physique, although he is slightly heavier than a true sighthound. There may be some Scottish Deerhound, as well – he's a large dog. His coat is very unusual, with that longer hair sticking up along his back, and that yields more clues to his origins. The grayish-white around his muzzle tells us that he's not a youngster. Older dogs can be great to adopt. They are house trained, and are often well-trained in general. And they're not as energetic as younger dogs, so even a large, athletic dog like this one can do well in an urban area.

Scottish Deerhound

EARS
Medium-sized rose ears, set high on the head and to the sides, are a sighthound feature.

Greyhound

Scottish Deerhound

HEAD
The long, narrow head is definitely sighthound. Like both hounds here, the widest point is between the ears and the head tapers down the muzzle, ending in a point at the nose.

Greyhound

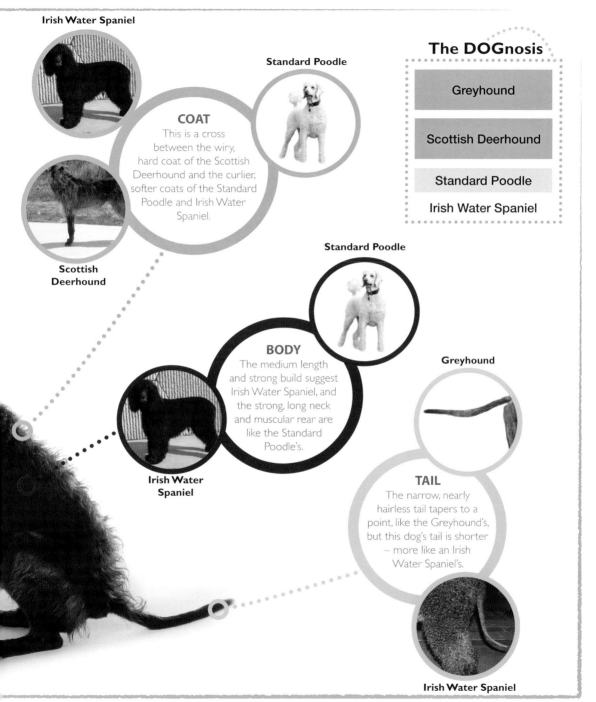

Irish Water Spaniel

Standard Poodle

COAT
This is a cross between the wiry, hard coat of the Scottish Deerhound and the curlier, softer coats of the Standard Poodle and Irish Water Spaniel.

Scottish Deerhound

The DOGnosis

Greyhound

Scottish Deerhound

Standard Poodle

Irish Water Spaniel

Standard Poodle

BODY
The medium length and strong build suggest Irish Water Spaniel, and the strong, long neck and muscular rear are like the Standard Poodle's.

Greyhound

Irish Water Spaniel

TAIL
The narrow, nearly hairless tail tapers to a point, like the Greyhound's, but this dog's tail is shorter – more like an Irish Water Spaniel's.

Irish Water Spaniel

Dobergrey Rottbeau

This dog looks a like a Doberman Pinscher crossed with a Rottweiler crossed with a Greyhound – and that's as good a guess as any. The Beauceron, a French herding and guard dog, has similar black and tan colouring, and is not as light as the Doberman nor as heavy as the Rottweiler. He may be in the mix, too. This is a strong, athletic dog. He will not run as fast as a Greyhound, but his over-all large size means he can still get where he's going quickly. He may tend to be strong-willed, but training will help him be a great companion.

HEAD
The long head resembles a blunt wedge, like a Doberman's, and is broad between the ears, with almond-shaped eyes, like a Rottweiler's.

Doberman Pinscher

Rottweiler

BODY
The long, athletic body and slightly arched neck are like the Greyhound's, but that broad, muscular chest is all Rottweiler.

Rottweiler

Greyhound

Doberman Pinscher

COAT
The short, smooth coat has the characteristic black background with clearly defined rust markings on the muzzle, paws, face and chest seen in all three breeds here.

Beauceron

Rottweiler

The DOGnosis

Doberman Pinscher

Greyhound

Beauceron

Rottweiler

Doberman Pinscher

EARS
The Doberman's ears are positioned high on the head and are of medium size, but they're dropped. These flying ears are a Greyhound trait.

Greyhound

Doberman Pinscher

PAWS AND LEGS
Long, straight front legs with smooth, long thighs and straight hocks (the area from the thigh to the ankle) resemble the Beauceron's. The feet are compact and not turned in or out, a Doberman trait.

Beauceron

131

Small Dogs

Manjack Chipin Terrier

Manchester Terrier

This sleek, sturdy, elegant little dog is a tiny terrier. His colouration suggests both Miniature Pinscher and Manchester Terrier. (The toy variety of the Manchester Terrier, by the way, is called the English Toy Terrier.) And there's a bit more substance about him that suggests the short-legged variety of the Jack Russell Terrier. What he lacks in size, he definitely makes up for in character. He is very lively and quite noisy too, proving to be an alert watchdog. This is the sort of little dog who is always jumping up to be where the action is. Don't make the mistake of neglecting to train him just because he's small.

HEAD
From the Jack Russell comes the distinct cheeks leading to a blunt-ended muzzle. The muzzle and skull are of equal length, like the Manchester Terrier's. And the Chihuahua contributes those large, round eyes.

Chihuahua

Jack Russell Terrier

Manchester Terrier

PAWS AND LEGS
Compact, round feet with well-arched toes are typical of the Manchester Terrier, while the front paws that turn slightly outwards are like the short-legged Jack Russell's.

Jack Russell Terrier

Manchester Terrier

Jack Russell Terrier

EARS
The Manchester's large ears are set high and back on the head, but the button ears are most likely from the toy variety of Manchester Terrier. The Jack Russell Terrier's ears are smaller and always drop down, but they fold all the way over.

Manchester Terrier

Chihuahua

BODY
Both the Manchester Terrier and the Chihuahua are a bit longer than they are tall. The Min Pin is compact, with a level topline and a well-developed chest.

Miniature Pinscher

COAT
The Min Pin's coat is smooth, short, dense, tight and glossy, and black and tan with a mask. But that white splash on the chest could be Chihuahua.

Chihuahua

Miniature Pinscher

The DOGnosis

| Manchester Terrier |
| Jack Russell Terrier |
| Miniature Pinscher |
| Chihuahua |

Manchester Ruggle Hund

There is definitely some terrier behind this very cute face: maybe the smooth-coated Manchester Terrier and the short-legged variety of the Jack Russell Terrier. But you can also see the Beagle in the black, tan and white colouring, and that long back brings the Dachshund to mind. This dog is a very lively character who displays great stamina and thrives on attention. Like many terrier types, he is not especially accommodating in the company of other dogs. Although he's small, he's no lap dog. If he has the opportunity to kill rats or mice, his hunting instincts will take over.

HEAD
The wedge-shaped long skull, with a visible narrowing from the end of the cheekbones to the start of the muzzle, is like the Jack Russell's. From the Beagle comes the domed top of the skull, with a broad area above the muzzle and wide-set eyes.

Jack Russell Terrier

Beagle

BODY
The long back and short legs, with a prominent chest, are Dachshund traits. The strong, solid, sturdy body with a muscular and moderately long neck are reminiscent of a Jack Russell's.

Dachshund

Jack Russell Terrier

Jack Russell Terrier

EARS
The Jack Russell Terrier has button ears set high on the head. The Manchester Terrier may have button ears or prick ears – either way, they're wide at the base and taper to pointed tips.

Manchester Terrier

The DOGnosis

Jack Russell Terrier

Beagle

Dachshund

Manchester Terrier

Manchester Terrier

Dachshund

COAT
The flat, hard, dense coat is characteristic of the Beagle, as is the tricolour pattern. The very rich, intense blacks and tans are likely from the Manchester Terrier.

Beagle

TAIL
Like the Dachshund's, the tail extends from the end of the spine and is long in relation to the dog's height. Like the Beagle's, it is carried up with a slight curve and has a little extra fur at the end.

Beagle

Aussietan Corgipin

Australian Cattle Dog

This dog's most striking characteristic is his large ears, but equally important are the shape of his face and his well-furred tail. All three make us think of the Corgi – the Cardigan Welsh Corgi in particular. (There are two types of Corgis: Pembroke Welsh Corgi and Cardigan Welsh Corgi. In this case, the Cardigan is more likely because this dog has a tail, unlike the Pembroke, and a tricoloured coat.) The relatively short legs and long body, plus the head shape, also suggest an Australian Cattle Dog. Both are bold dogs who are not easily intimidated. This is a reflection of the work they were bred for: snapping at the heels of reluctant cattle to encourage them to move.

HEAD
This is the general shape of a Corgi's head, with wide cheeks set into a strong, short neck, but the skull and muzzle of this dog are not as long as the Corgi's. For overall head size and muzzle length, the Australian Cattle Dog is a better match.

Corgi

BODY
The short, strong body, moderately short neck and good depth of ribs all suggest a Tibetan Spaniel. The body is longer than it is tall, but the legs are still fairly long, like the Australian Cattle Dog's.

Australian Cattle Dog

Tibetan Spaniel

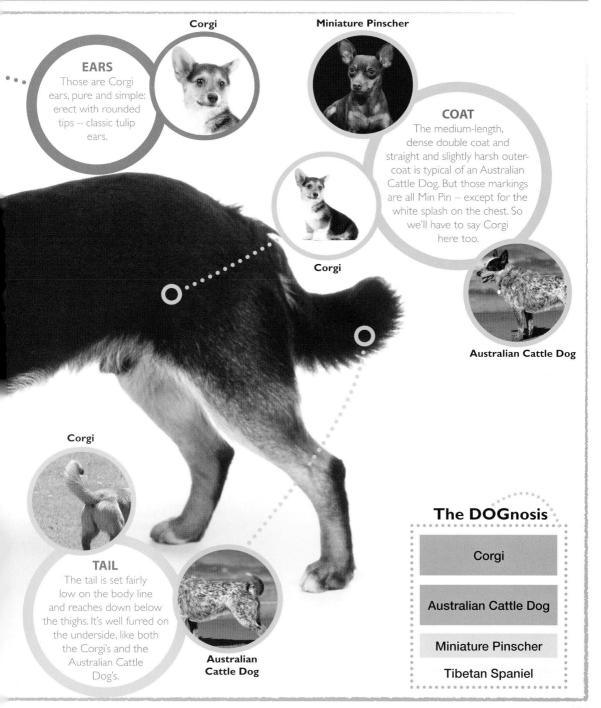

Corgi

Miniature Pinscher

EARS
Those are Corgi ears, pure and simple: erect with rounded tips – classic tulip ears.

COAT
The medium-length, dense double coat and straight and slightly harsh outer-coat is typical of an Australian Cattle Dog. But those markings are all Min Pin – except for the white splash on the chest. So we'll have to say Corgi here too.

Corgi

Australian Cattle Dog

Corgi

The DOGnosis

Corgi
Australian Cattle Dog
Miniature Pinscher
Tibetan Spaniel

TAIL
The tail is set fairly low on the body line and reaches down below the thighs. It's well furred on the underside, like both the Corgi's and the Australian Cattle Dog's.

Australian Cattle Dog

Tibetan Jackpuchi

The smooth coat and broad skull on this dog point to her being part Chihuahua, which helps to explain her rather excitable nature and the way she may start shivering when she is excited or simply nervous. There is also some terrier in her past, with Jack Russell Terrier stock almost certainly being involved, as reflected in her colour and pattern. But she's a solid little dog, and that suggests a thicker-set toy breed, such as a Pug, also played a role in her ancestry. There are also some similarities to a Tibetan Spaniel – a dog described as 'assertive.' In fact, this dog has a rather dominant nature, despite her small stature, as may become evident when she meets larger dogs. Early socialization and good training will help with that problem.

Tibetan Spaniel

HEAD
The top of the skull is wide and domed, like a Chihuahua's, with a medium blunt muzzle, like a Tibetan Spaniel's – a dog whose head is also small in proportion to the body.

Chihuahua

PAWS AND LEGS
Very strong legs of moderate length, set directly under the body, like a Pug's, with strong hindquarters and hare feet (long toes), like a Tibetan Spaniel's.

Pug

Tibetan Spaniel

Pug

Tibetan Spaniel

The DOGnosis

Chihuahua

Jack Russell Terrier

Tibetan Spaniel

Pug

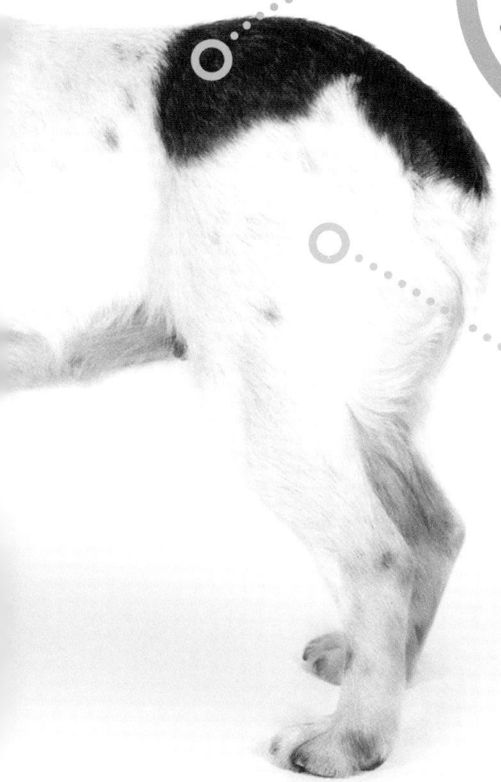

EARS
These are a cross between the medium, V-shaped ears of the Tibetan Spaniel (which hang down) and the small, soft, folded ears of the Pug.

COAT
The Chihuahua's coat is smooth, close to the body and glossy, with a ruff on the neck. But the colour and markings are all Jack Russell.

Chihuahua

Jack Russell Terrier

Pug

BODY
The Pug is short in the back and wide in the chest, the Chihuahua is slightly longer than tall and the Tibetan Spaniel has a short, strong neck and arched ribs.

Chihuahua

Tibetan Spaniel

Labrador Bachshund

This is a small dog with a big dog look – the not-quite-Labrador Retriever head and neck see to that. His short, stocky legs support a relatively long body, which, combined with the smooth coat and the way in which his front feet are slightly angled, suggest a Dachshund lurks somewhere in his past. The narrowing of the face is another clue – although there may be a bit of the Jack Russell Terrier in that, especially the ears. Jack Russells sometimes have short legs as well. And there might be a little scenthound in his background, contributing the white markings on his otherwise black coat. This is a very active dog, despite his small size.

HEAD
Wide skull with powerful jaws, suggesting a Labrador Retriever, but a little bit domed with a tapering, slightly blunt muzzle that is not pointy, like a Jack Russell's.

Labrador Retriever

Jack Russell Terrier

Jack Russell Terrier

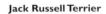

PAWS AND LEGS
Short legs with relatively large paws and no wrinkling on the skin. The slight inward curve on the front legs is especially suggestive of a Dachshund.

Dachshund

EARS

Set well-back on the head and not large or heavy, like a Beagle's, but held out and folded, like a Jack Russell's.

Beagle

Labrador Retriever

Jack Russell Terrier

COAT

Short, glossy, dense and black, like the Labrador Retriever's, with just a hint of white on the chest that suggests Beagle.

Beagle

Dachshund

BODY

Longer than tall, like a Dachshund, but the round shape, level back and strong neck suggest a Lab.

Labrador Retriever

The DOGnosis

| Labrador Retriever |
| Dachshund |
| Beagle |
| Jack Russell Terrier |

Corgidach Brithund

This dog's rich chestnut and white coat suggests the likelihood of some hunting dog ancestry, possibly a Brittany. This is reinforced by his friendly nature and the longer hair – called feathering – on his legs and tail, which is a feature seen in many hunting breeds, including spaniels. His short legs and long body suggest there could also be some Dachshund blood lurking in his ancestry – the long-haired variety may have contributed to his flat, wavy coat, as well. But his head is more a like a dog who has a similar body shape – the Corgi – with a cute pair of spaniel ears (the Brittany influence again). His spaniel and herding dog heritage (that's the Corgi) mean he is energetic. He'll thrive on long walks, where his broad nose will help him to detect a wide range of interesting scents. His short legs mean he'll be able to follow that scent under and into just about anything.

HEAD
Moderate size with a broad forehead suggests Corgi, but the tapering muzzle shows a hint of Dachshund.

Corgi

Dachshund

Dachshund

Corgi

BODY
Short legs, long body, with a slight arch towards the rear – could be from either the Dachshund or the Corgi.

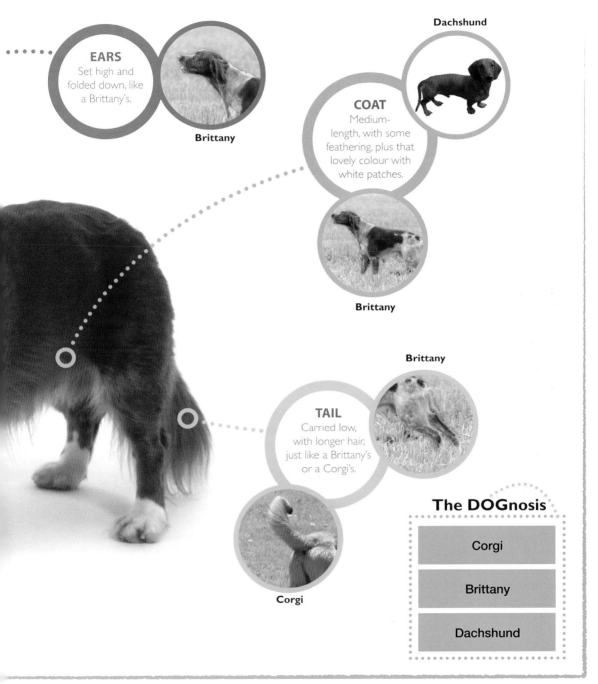

EARS
Set high and folded down, like a Brittany's.

Brittany

Dachshund

COAT
Medium-length, with some feathering, plus that lovely colour with white patches.

Brittany

Brittany

TAIL
Carried low, with longer hair, just like a Brittany's or a Corgi's.

Corgi

The DOGnosis

Corgi
Brittany
Dachshund

Pomhond

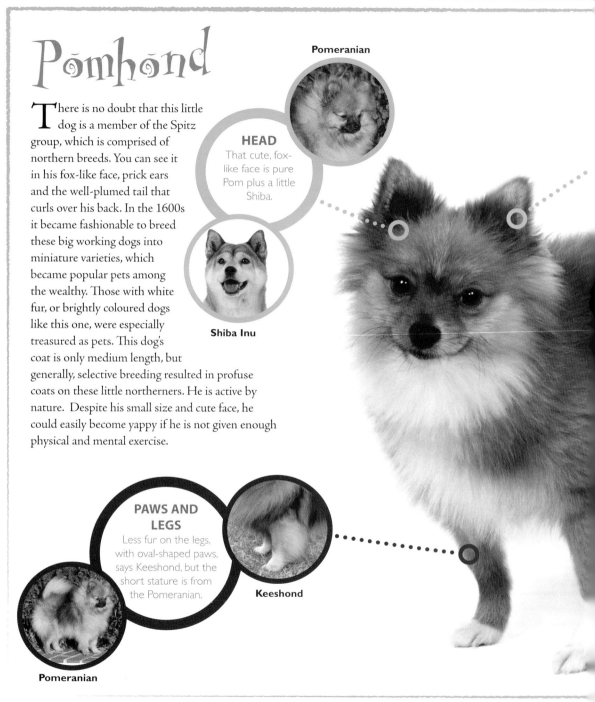

There is no doubt that this little dog is a member of the Spitz group, which is comprised of northern breeds. You can see it in his fox-like face, prick ears and the well-plumed tail that curls over his back. In the 1600s it became fashionable to breed these big working dogs into miniature varieties, which became popular pets among the wealthy. Those with white fur, or brightly coloured dogs like this one, were especially treasured as pets. This dog's coat is only medium length, but generally, selective breeding resulted in profuse coats on these little northerners. He is active by nature. Despite his small size and cute face, he could easily become yappy if he is not given enough physical and mental exercise.

Pomeranian

HEAD
That cute, fox-like face is pure Pom plus a little Shiba.

Shiba Inu

PAWS AND LEGS
Less fur on the legs, with oval-shaped paws, says Keeshond, but the short stature is from the Pomeranian.

Keeshond

Pomeranian

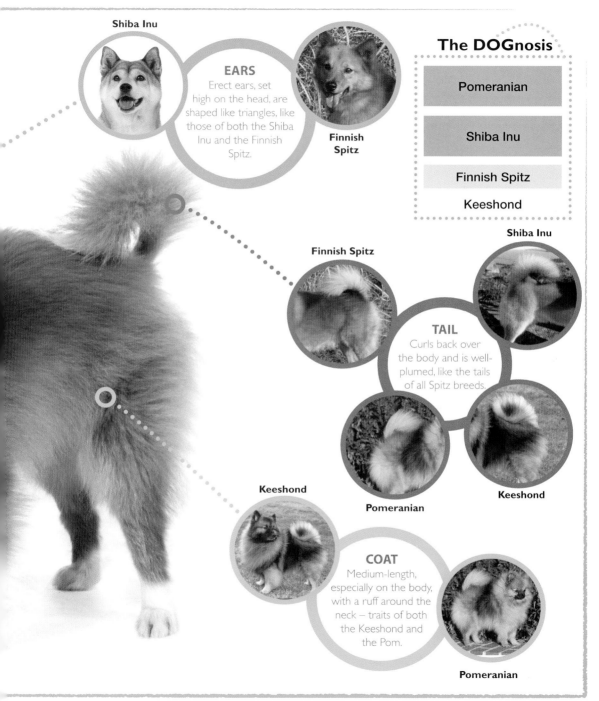

Shiba Inu

EARS
Erect ears, set high on the head, are shaped like triangles, like those of both the Shiba Inu and the Finnish Spitz.

Finnish Spitz

The DOGnosis

Pomeranian

Shiba Inu

Finnish Spitz

Keeshond

Finnish Spitz

Shiba Inu

TAIL
Curls back over the body and is well-plumed, like the tails of all Spitz breeds.

Pomeranian

Keeshond

Keeshond

COAT
Medium-length, especially on the body, with a ruff around the neck – traits of both the Keeshond and the Pom.

Pomeranian

147

Pappy King Spaniel

Toy spaniels of various types have been kept as companions for centuries. This little boy is a descendant of these delightful pets and has the friendly, affectionate nature you'd expect from a dog who has experienced centuries of aristocratic living and being the centre of attention. His colours and markings say Papillon and Cavalier King Charles Spaniel. His ears are another giveaway: the long hair is pure Papillon, but the fact that they droop says Cavalier King Charles. His head is large and his body is quite stocky – another hint of the Cavalier, with possibly a Jack Russell Terrier in the mix. Miniature spaniels are still hunting dogs at heart, so they're active and easy to train.

Cavalier King Charles Spaniel

HEAD
Tapering, but not to a point, with strong, medium-length jaws.

Jack Russell Terrier

COAT
Medium-length, wavy and profuse; likely inherited from the Cavalier or Papillon. The mostly white colour and symmetrical head markings are also typical of those two breeds.

Cavalier King Charles Spaniel

Papillon

EARS

Set quite high, with longer hair, says Papillon, but they drop like a true spaniel's.

Cavalier King Charles Spaniel

Papillon

The DOGnosis

Papillon

Cavalier King Charles Spaniel

Jack Russell Terrier

Jack Russell Terrier

BODY

Broad-chested and square, giving the impression of strength.

Cavalier King Charles Spaniel

PAWS AND LEGS

Short, sturdy, wide-set legs are typical of the Jack Russell Terrier, while the round feet are from the Cavalier.

Cavalier King Charles Spaniel

Jack Russell Terrier

Chipomlapp

Short in stature but not in character, this is a toy dog with a very international heritage. You can see the Mexican Chihuahua influence in his head and the German Pomeranian and/or Swedish Lapphund in his overall look. (The likelihood of Lapphund depends on where he was born.) But then you've got that compact, square little body with the broad chest – highly indicative of a Pug (which originated in China). Put them all together and you've got both a lively little companion and probably a noisy watchdog, as well: a big dog in a little dog's body.

Pomeranian

TAIL
Curls over the back, like those of the Pomeranian and the Lapphund – both northern breeds – and also like the Pug's.

Pug

Swedish Lapphund

Chihuahua

Pug

COAT
Short and smooth but with some length in places, this coat is a happy medium between the longer-haired Pom and Lapphund and the shorter-haired Chihuahua and Pug. The black colour suggests Lapphund or Pug.

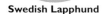
Swedish Lapphund

Pomeranian

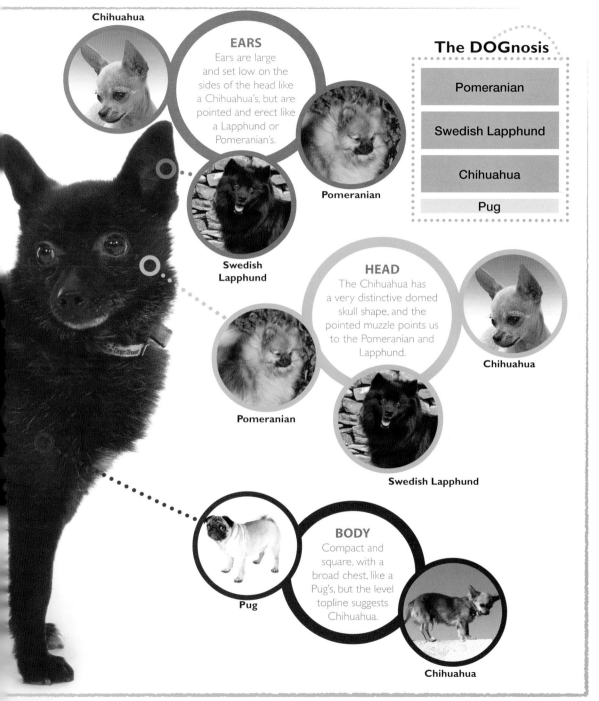

Chihuahua

EARS
Ears are large and set low on the sides of the head like a Chihuahua's, but are pointed and erect like a Lapphund or Pomeranian's.

Pomeranian

Swedish Lapphund

The DOGnosis

Pomeranian

Swedish Lapphund

Chihuahua

Pug

HEAD
The Chihuahua has a very distinctive domed skull shape, and the pointed muzzle points us to the Pomeranian and Lapphund.

Chihuahua

Pomeranian

Swedish Lapphund

BODY
Compact and square, with a broad chest, like a Pug's, but the level topline suggests Chihuahua.

Pug

Chihuahua

Bearded Australian YorkiePoo

This girl is the kind of mutt best known as 'scruffy little dog'. There are a few obvious influences in her make-up, some that are not so obvious and others that will forever be a mystery. In some ways she is like a Bearded Collie, especially in terms of her overall proportions. There are some significant differences though, such as her shorter coat, that suggest another herding breed, perhaps an Australian Shepherd. And a Yorkshire Terrier can't be ruled out, based on the small, hairy, prick ears. There is something of the Poodle about her coat, too – when you remember that not all Poodle crosses end up with curly hair. About the only thing we know for sure is that this dog will need plenty of grooming!

Bearded Collie

HEAD
Broad and rounded, with a short, square muzzle and a large nose: Bearded Collie all the way.

Yorkshire Terrier

Australian Shepherd

PAWS AND LEGS
Dainty yet hairy paws are the Poodle's contribution (or the Yorkie's), while the well-boned front legs and broad, muscular hindquarters are Sheltie traits.

Miniature Poodle

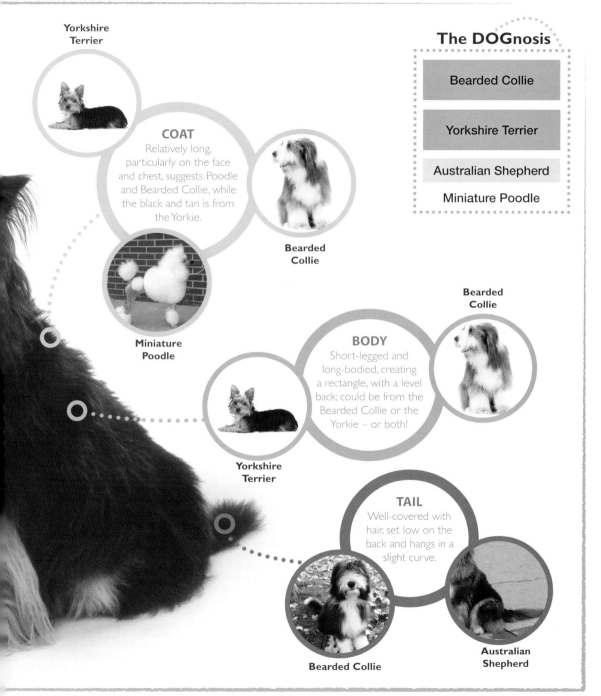

Yorkshire
Terrier

The DOGnosis

Bearded Collie

Yorkshire Terrier

Australian Shepherd

Miniature Poodle

COAT
Relatively long,
particularly on the face
and chest, suggests Poodle
and Bearded Collie, while
the black and tan is from
the Yorkie.

Bearded
Collie

Miniature
Poodle

Bearded
Collie

BODY
Short-legged and
long-bodied, creating
a rectangle, with a level
back; could be from the
Bearded Collie or the
Yorkie – or both!

Yorkshire
Terrier

TAIL
Well-covered with
hair; set low on the
back and hangs in a
slight curve.

Bearded Collie

Australian
Shepherd

Basspei Pughund

It is obvious this is not one of the giants of the dog world. Her short legs suggest that probably a Basset Hound played a significant role, but everything else is up for grabs – especially the ears! The black mask on her face is quite distinctive, possibly passed on from a Pug. But, depending on her precise origins, there may even be a hint of that other Chinese breed, the Shar-Pei, in her ancestry. If you're having a hard time imagining a Shar-Pei and a Basset Hound getting together, remember that most mutts are the result of dozens of crosses over many generations. This is an active little dog with a sweet nature and a lot of spirit.

HEAD
A domed, quite broad skull with a wide muzzle and some wrinkling on the forehead.

Shar-Pei

Basset Hound

Dachshund

PAWS AND LEGS
Short, with the paws somewhat at an angle, like those of both a Dachshund and Basset Hound. The feet are big, too, like a Basset's.

Basset Hound

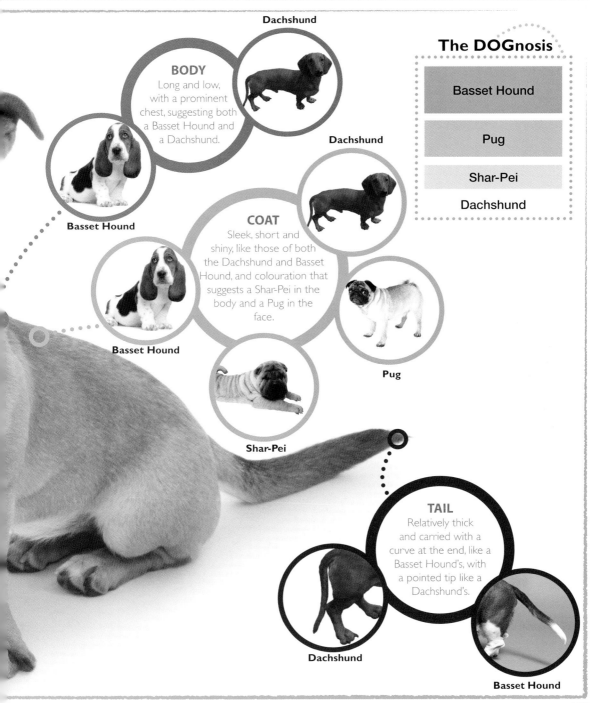

Dachshund

BODY
Long and low, with a prominent chest, suggesting both a Basset Hound and a Dachshund.

Basset Hound

Dachshund

COAT
Sleek, short and shiny, like those of both the Dachshund and Basset Hound, and colouration that suggests a Shar-Pei in the body and a Pug in the face.

Basset Hound

Pug

Shar-Pei

The DOGnosis

Basset Hound
Pug
Shar-Pei

Dachshund

TAIL
Relatively thick and carried with a curve at the end, like a Basset Hound's, with a pointed tip like a Dachshund's.

Dachshund

Basset Hound

Bullagle Mounterrier

It's really difficult to classify this dog. His overall look suggests a little bit of everything. He's slender in some parts and wide in others. He's small overall, but he has a big-dog look. He looks like a scenthound, a terrier and a larger breed of working dog. With all this in the mix, he is an alert guardian, with strong protective instincts for those people who are in his immediate circle. He's inquisitive, and needs plenty of toys and exercise to keep him out of trouble. He can be quite noisy, too (that's the Beagle in him), and will bark to express his excitement or his concerns about strangers. He may also bark simply when he wants attention.

Beagle

HEAD
The long, domed skull is very much like a Beagle's. But the tapering wedge shape, with a slight break between the forehead and the muzzle, suggests a Manchester Terrier.

Manchester Terrier

PAWS AND LEGS
The Beagle has straight legs with plenty of strength, and the French Bulldog's muscular legs are set wide apart with the feet facing slightly outward.

French Bulldog

Beagle

Manchester Terrier

EARS

Somewhere between the large V-shaped erect ears of the Manchester Terrier and the triangular drop ears of the Greater Swiss Mountain Dog are these semi-drop ears. Dogs like the Swissie do raise and bring their ears forward when they're excited.

The DOGnosis

Beagle

French Bulldog

Manchester Terrier

Greater Swiss Mountain Dog

Greater Swiss Mountain Dog

COAT

The overall colouration suggests Beagle and Greater Swiss Mountain Dog. The texture is also like both breeds: a hard, close, dense coat of medium length.

Greater Swiss Mountain Dog

Beagle

Beagle

BODY

This dog's back is short, muscular and strong like a Beagle's, and he has a very broad, strong, flat chest like a French Bulldog.

French Bulldog

157

Hunting Dogs

Chezsla Hound Retriever

This dog looks like a Labrador Retriever in an unusual colour, but there's no doubt about his Lab ancestors. The colour is a bit like the brown, or sedge, of a Chesapeake Bay Retriever, and a bit like the Vizsla's rusty red. The two retrievers in his make-up mean he loves to swim, and he'll also be a dependable, easily trained companion. The areas of white, the rounded skull and the smaller feet suggest the contribution of a large scenthound, as well. Depending on where you live, it might be reflective of a Foxhound or a Hamiltonstovare, a Swedish scenthound.

Labrador Retriever

HEAD
The wide skull, powerful jaws and blunt muzzle are from the Labrador Retriever and the rounded dome atop the skull says scenthound.

Hamiltonstovare

Foxhound

Foxhound

PAWS AND LEGS
The medium-length, straight legs are not too thick, suggesting the Chessie, while the narrow paws with long toes splashed with white fur are from the hounds.

Hamiltonstovare

Chesapeake Bay Retriever

EARS

Large drop ears are set behind the eyes on the sides of the head, like a hound's, and hang down and frame the face, like a Lab's.

Labrador Retriever

Hamiltonstovare

The DOGnosis

Labrador Retriever
Foxhound/ Hamiltonstovare
Chesapeake Bay Retriever
Vizsla

Chesapeake Bay Retriever

TAIL

The tail is thick along its length, well-furred and tapers from the root to the tip – a classic retriever trait called an otter tail.

Labrador Retriever

Chesapeake Bay Retriever

Vizsla

COAT

The coat is short, water-resistant and dense, like those of both retrievers, with Vizsla colour and hound markings on the chest, face and feet.

Foxhound

Hamiltonstovare

Vizslaraner

This is a strong, well-built dog with a variety of hunting breeds in his background plus, probably, a little bit of sighthound. It's the ears and the slighter profile of his body that suggest a hound ancestor. He is an exuberant, confident dog and will make a great family companion. Crossing hunting dogs with hounds was once fairly common, to get a working companion who also had superior speed. In the old days, these dogs were not called mutts – they were just hunting dogs with all the right qualities.

Weimaraner

HEAD
The shape of the skull, which tapers just a bit, and the muzzle, which is wide and rounded on top, are like a Weimaraner's. Like a Lab's, the skull is wide between the ears, the cheeks are well-defined but not fleshy and the flews (the lips) are tight but extend just below the jaw.

Labrador Retriever

Vizsla

PAWS AND LEGS
The front legs are long and straight and the muscular hind legs are relatively straight, like a Vizsla's. Those Whippet feet are compact, but the toes are a little longer than in our other breeds.

Whippet

Weimaraner

EARS

The set of the ears, high and to the sides of the head, suggests Weimaraner, but the propeller ears come from a Whippet.

Whippet

The DOGnosis

Vizsla
Weimaraner
Labrador Retriever

Whippet

BODY

The Weimaraner has a moderately long body with a level back. The Vizsla has a relatively broad, deep chest for such a slim dog, with a slight tuck-up at the tummy.

Vizsla

Weimaraner

Vizsla

COAT

The rust colour indicates the Vizsla. But the coat is a little harder and longer, suggesting a Labrador Retriever. The small spot of white on the chest is also sometimes seen in Labs.

Labrador Retriever

Pointy Dalhound

What an interesting and attractive mix this dog is! There's a German Shorthaired Pointer head, Dalmatian colouring with English Setter-style speckling and the lithe body of a Greyhound. That smooth coat means grooming is very straightforward; stroking the coat with a special grooming glove should maintain his immaculate appearance. However, those short hairs are stiff and tend to stick in upholstered furniture. This is an active dog and may not be well-suited to a life in a small urban flat. Regular daily walks and runs, rather than weekend marathons, are essential, to prevent him from becoming bored and destructive.

HEAD
Slightly domed, with a broad skull and a deep, straight, blunt muzzle, like a German Shorthaired Pointer's. The head is set on a fairly long, nicely arched neck, like a Dalmatian's.

Dalmatian

German Shorthaired Pointer

PAWS AND LEGS
Small, close-knit feet with arched toes suggest German Shorthaired Pointer; while the straight, sturdy front legs with elbows close to the body, and very smooth yet strong thighs, are Dalmatian traits.

Dalmatian

German Shorthaired Pointer

Dalmatian

BODY
The Dalmatian has a chest that's deep but not broad, and the rib cage reaches well down. The Greyhound has the same type of chest, but a more lithe body and a tuck-up underneath.

Greyhound

COAT
The short, thick, smooth coat, coloured white with black spots and blotches, is the hallmark of the Dalmatian. But the speckled black and white pattern is more like an English Setter's.

English Setter

Dalmatian

TAIL
The medium-length, tapering tail is a natural extension of the dog's topline – a characteristic of both the Dalmatian and the English Setter.

English Setter

Dalmatian

Retrieving Husky Hound

There is little doubt that this dog's ancestry includes some hunting dog genes. His colour and build suggest both Golden and Labrador Retriever. But he is clearly lighter in his body, suggesting a hound cross – possibly a Greyhound. His sleek coat and the position and shape of his ears are also like those of a sighthound. He is more active than a retriever, as well, and is able to sprint surprisingly fast. He'll have to be discouraged from chasing cats. The northern Husky heritage is evident in his tail and his white underside. All in all, this is a good family pet with a gentle, supportive nature.

Labrador Retriever

HEAD
The wide skull with a broad nose is a Labrador Retriever's, but the tapering shape from the forehead to the muzzle suggests Husky.

Siberian Husky

Labrador Retriever

BODY
This dog is longer than he is tall, with a stocky profile and deep chest suggestive of both retrievers, but his overall lightness is from the Greyhound.

Greyhound

Golden Retriever

EARS
These are called propeller ears and they are sometimes found on some sighthounds, including the Greyhound.

Labrador Retriever

TAIL
Thick and sturdy like a Labrador Retriever's, but heavily furred underneath and carried in a gentle curl, like a Husky's.

The DOGnosis

Labrador Retriever
Siberian Husky
Golden Retriever

Greyhound

Greyhound

Siberian Husky

Labrador Retriever

COAT
Relatively short and sleek like a Greyhound's, the colour and density of a yellow Lab's and the white underside and mask of a Husky.

Greyhound

Siberian Husky

167

Loxer Bull Retriever

The brindle pattern on this dog's coat, with black lines running like waves through a rich chestnut-red background, is especially striking. He is a stocky dog, even though he is not yet fully grown, and will be a big adult. He is clearly from working dog stock, and therefore has quite a strong, determined temperament. He also has a bit of an independent streak, but, like all dogs bred to do a job, he responds well to training. He's going to need plenty of exercise and probably loves a good swim – evidence of a retrieving instinct.

Boxer

BODY
Stocky and muscular overall. The long back is like a Boxer's, while the dip behind the top of the shoulders suggests Bullmastiff.

Bullmastiff

PAWS AND LEGS
Very strong front legs with pronounced wrists and long, powerful thighs come from the Bullmastiff. The large, round paws are like a Lab's.

Labrador Retriever

Bullmastiff

Boxer

HEAD

The broad, square skull suggests Boxer, and the long but blocky muzzle is like the Labrador Retriever's.

Labrador Retriever

The DOGnosis

Boxer
Labrador Retriever
Bullmastiff

EARS

V-shaped ears, set high on the head and dropped over, suggest Bullmastiff, but the length and the rounded tips are more like a Lab's ears.

Bullmastiff

Labrador Retriever

COAT

The smooth, short coat with the brindle pattern could be Boxer or Bullmastiff, and the glossy sheen and dense texture are Labrador heritage.

Labrador Retriever

Boxer

Bullmastiff

169

Labra-Coat Foxtriever

The glossy coat and the head of this dog clearly reveal that a Labrador Retriever played a role in his ancestry. Nevertheless, he is more lightly built than a purebred Labrador Retriever. There are likely some other hunting dogs in his background, and possibly even a hound, such as the Foxhound. Friendly and lively by nature, this dog is an ideal companion in a home with older children, since he will have as much energy as they do. His keen retrieving instincts mean that he is always ready to play – especially fetch. He may not be well-suited to urban life, though, because he needs a lot of exercise. He is also something of a glutton, and requires plenty of opportunity to burn off the calories so he doesn't become overweight.

Weimaraner

HEAD
Broad head with a flat top, with nicely chiselled cheekbones and a blocky muzzle.

Labrador Retriever

BODY
Strong and well-proportioned, with a powerful chest, like a Lab, but not as wide and chunky as a typical Lab.

Labrador Retriever

Foxhound

Foxhound

PAWS AND LEGS
Strong, thick legs from the Lab, straight front legs with well-arched toes from the Foxhound.

Labrador Retriever

The DOGnosis

Labrador Retriever

Flat-Coated Retriever

Foxhound

Weimaraner

Labrador Retriever

EARS
Large, set on the top and sides of the head, and hanging down, like those of both retrievers.

Flat-Coated Retriever

Labrador Retriever

COAT
The short, glossy parts are the Lab's heritage, while the longer parts and the hard texture, plus the colour, say Flat-Coat.

Flat-Coated Retriever

Pointing Greydane

The striking speckled pattern and body shape on this girl suggests some Pointer ancestry. Pointers find game with their nose, and that long, broad muzzle is just the right tool. But her head has a gentler slope from forehead to muzzle and those ears – well, you'd never find them on a Pointer! There seems to be a little bit of the hound in this dog, too; you can see it in the tucked-up tummy and the tail held down between her hind legs. Sighthounds hunt by following game visually. A dog like this, with two kinds of hunters in her heritage, is likely to be serious and hardworking. She is also big and energetic, and will need plenty of exercise. Give her a job to do and you'll find she's smart and easy to train. But if she gets bored, she could become destructive.

HEAD
Long, broad muzzle with loose lips suggests Pointer or Great Dane. The gently sloping forehead is all Dane.

Pointer

Great Dane

Greyhound

BODY
The topline slopes down to the hindquarters, with a tucked-up tummy like a Greyhound's but a broad, full chest like a Pointer's.

Pointer

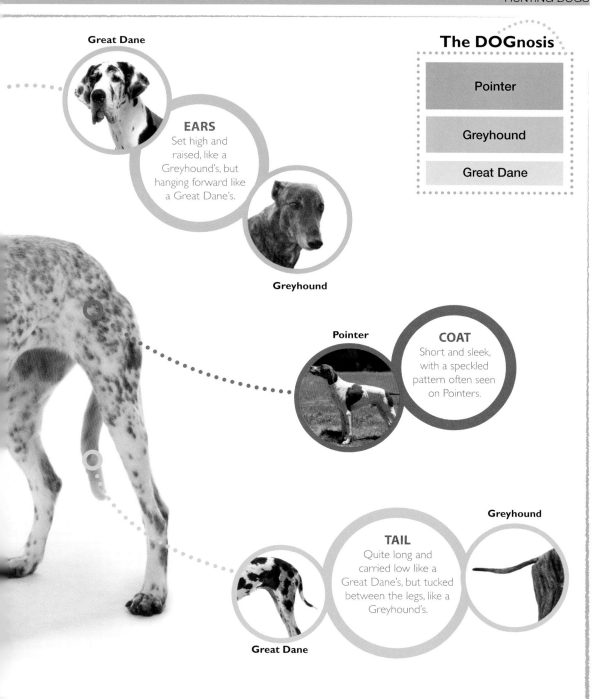

Great Dane

EARS
Set high and raised, like a Greyhound's, but hanging forward like a Great Dane's.

Greyhound

The DOGnosis

Pointer

Greyhound

Great Dane

Pointer

COAT
Short and sleek, with a speckled pattern often seen on Pointers.

Greyhound

TAIL
Quite long and carried low like a Great Dane's, but tucked between the legs, like a Greyhound's.

Great Dane

Danish SetPoint

This dog seems to be part Pointer, although his head is broader and his ears are very different. He is a tall dog, and his black and white colouring helps provide another clue about his ancestry: he probably also has a Great Dane ancestor with the black and white pattern known as harlequin. His coat, with just a little something extra around the neck, suggests a hint of English Setter as well. Despite his large size, this boy is a very amenable individual, and his sleek coat means that little time has to be spent on grooming. Even so, his large appetite means feeding him can be an expensive proposition.

Pointer

HEAD
Broad and cleanly chiselled, with a long, rectangular muzzle – the Pointer and Great Dane are likely responsible.

Great Dane

BODY
This dog is as long as he is tall, like the Pointer and the Great Dane.

Pointer

Great Dane

PAWS AND LEGS
Long, straight forelegs say Pointer, while the tight, strong feet and speckled legs are from the English Setter.

English Setter

Pointer

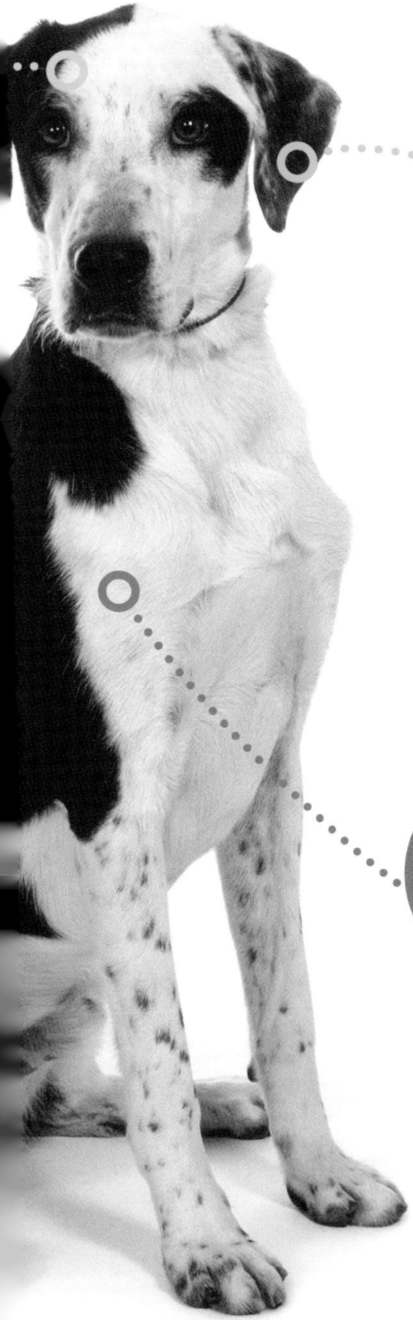

The DOGnosis

Pointer
Great Dane
English Setter

EARS
Relatively large, set towards the back of the skull, high set and folded over – it all says Great Dane.

Great Dane

COAT
Short and quite sleek says Pointer, but the pattern looks inherited from a harlequin Great Dane and that little bit of fluff is most likely from the Setter.

Pointer

Great Dane

English Setter

Goldepeake Shepherd

One look at that body and you know there's a Golden Retriever somewhere in this dog's lineage. But her head tells another story. She lacks the square muzzle and the drop ears that are typical of retrievers. No, that head says herding dog. Maybe a Collie with those ears? Maybe a German Shepherd with that muzzle? And although we are used to seeing German Shepherds in black and brown, they do come in other colours. Whatever the specifics, retriever and shepherd is a winning combination: smart, easily trained, social and good with kids.

HEAD
Large and triangular, with a strong, tapering muzzle; a German Shepherd is the most likely ancestor.

German Shepherd

PAWS AND LEGS
The strong limbs and large paws of a retriever – a dog born to swim.

Golden Retriever

Chesapeake Bay Retriever

German Shepherd

EARS
Triangular and high on the head, like a German Shepherd's, but dropping at the tips, like a Collie's.

Collie

The DOGnosis

Golden Retriever

German Shepherd

Chesapeake Bay Retriever

Collie

Golden Retriever

BODY
The long, strong back that is slightly rounded over the rear is characteristic of retrievers.

Chesapeake Bay Retriever

Golden Retriever

COAT
Golden and flat but wavy – that's all retriever. The heavy feathering underneath and on the tail tells a different story, though.

Collie

Designer Dogs

Labradoodle

Figuring out which breeds are in a mutt's background is always something of a guess. But these so-called designer dogs are the result of two lines of purebred dogs being mated, with the aim of establishing new types of dogs with predictable characteristics. The Labradoodle is a very popular example. He was first bred in the 1980s in Australia when a woman who needed a guide dog asked for one who would not irritate her husband's allergy to dogs. Still, this is not a hypoallergenic dog – Poodles just shed less. And he's just as active and smart as both 'founder' breeds.

HEAD
The wide skull, with plenty of space between the ears, and a wide nose, is from the Lab. The moderately rounded top and the long, straight, strong muzzle are Poodle characteristics.

Labrador Retriever

Standard Poodle

BODY
The Lab has a powerful build with a level topline. The Poodle has a deep and moderately wide chest and a rear that is broad, short and muscular.

Labrador Retriever

Standard Poodle

PAWS AND LEGS
The Lab has very strong, thick legs with large, compact feet and thick foot pads. The Poodle has long, straight legs, front and back.

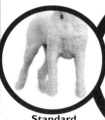

Standard Poodle

Labrador Retriever

Labrador Retriever

| Labrador Retriever |
| Standard Poodle |

Standard Poodle

EARS

These are mostly Poodle ears – long and furry, set low and hanging close to the head. But Lab ears are also set low and hang close, and the shorter hair keeps these ears manageable.

Labrador Retriever

COAT

This dog has a fleece coat, which hangs in loose, loopy spirals. It's a combination of the harsh, curly, dense coat of the Poodle and the flat, hard, short coat of the Lab.

Standard Poodle

Labrador Retriever

TAIL

The tail is quite thick at the base and tapers, like a Lab's. It's set high up on the back, carried high and well-furred, like a Poodle's.

Standard Poodle

Puggle

Puggles are the progeny of Pugs and Beagles, and they seem to have gotten the best of both. Everything that is extreme in the Pug and the Beagle is offered in moderation in the Puggle. This is an energetic little hound with the playfulness of a companion dog. They are social and affectionate, and are a bit easier to train than the typical Beagle. They will enjoy their exercise, but will also accept a good cuddle. And they get along well with children, other dogs and most other pets. However, they do retain that Beagle tendency to bark and howl.

Pug

HEAD

The slightly domed skull and distinct muzzle is from the Beagle, while the large, round shape and wrinkled forehead is from the Pug.

Beagle

Pug

BODY

This is basically a Pug body: compact and thickset, with lots of depth in the ribs. The Beagle adds a little length in the back and a longer neck.

Beagle

Beagle

PAWS AND LEGS

The strong, straight legs of moderate length are traits of both breeds, but the feet that are not quite round and not quite long are from the Pug.

Pug

The DOGnosis

Pug

Beagle

EARS
A compromise between the two breeds. The Pug has small, thin, triangular, black ears that are button or rose in shape. The Beagle's ears are broader and bigger, and always hang down.

Pug

Beagle

TAIL
The tail is a bit thick and set quite high on the back, like both breeds. The gentle curl is the middle ground between the Beagle's straight tail and the Pug's tight double curl.

Beagle

Pug

COAT
Quite short, smooth and glossy, like both breeds. Most Puggles are fawn, a common Pug colour, but some are tan, black, white or tricoloured, like the Beagle.

Beagle

Pug

Cockapoo

The Cockapoo is a Poodle-Cocker Spaniel cross. Poodles of all three sizes (Standard, Miniature and Toy) may appear in her ancestry, as may both English and American Cocker Spaniels. The result is a dog who comes in several sizes but always has the cuddly look and super intelligence of the Poodle, and the patient disposition and sturdy build of the Cocker Spaniel. The resulting dog is very focused on her family, good with children, friendly with strangers, active but not hyper and relatively easier to groom than either of her parent breeds. In Australia and northern Europe, these dogs are called Spoodles.

HEAD
Like a Cocker Spaniel's, the length of the muzzle just about matches the length of the skull and the muzzle is not pointed. Like a Poodle's, the head is rounded on top and the face is broad with dark, wide-set eyes.

Miniature Poodle

Cocker Spaniel

BODY
The square body shape in profile and level back are Poodle traits. The well-built, solid appearance and wide chest are from the Cocker Spaniel.

Cocker Spaniel

Miniature Poodle

Miniature Poodle

PAWS AND LEGS
Straight front legs and wide, muscular hips are Cocker Spaniel traits. The delicate, oval feet are from the Poodle.

Cocker Spaniel

Cocker Spaniel

EARS

The ears are set low on the head and are long, like the Cocker Spaniel's. They hang down close to the head and are covered with curly hair, like the Poodle's.

Miniature Poodle

The DOGnosis

Miniature Poodle
Cocker Spaniel

Miniature Poodle

COAT

The Cocker Spaniel's coat is short and fine on the head, longer on the body and straight. The Poodle's coat is curly and dense. This dog has a bit of both.

Cocker Spaniel

TAIL

The Poodle's tail is straight, high set and completely covered in hair. The Cocker's tail tends to be carried horizontally, sometimes higher.

Cocker Spaniel

Miniature Poodle

Schnoodle

This Schnoodle is a cross between a Miniature Schnauzer and a Miniature Poodle. Because Poodles come in three sizes and Schnauzers come in two, you can find much bigger Schnoodles and slightly smaller ones. They all inherit the intelligence of both ancestral breeds and tend to be very focused on the people in their family. They like to learn and they love to play games. They also like to run – but since they're small, you don't need to take them jogging all afternoon to tire them out. Their coat does not shed as much as other breeds, but grows continuously. This requires weekly brushing and a trim every two or three months to make sure matting does not become an issue.

HEAD

On the Schnauzer, the top part of the skull is long but the muzzle is not too long and ends bluntly. The wide face, very dark eyes set wide apart and moderately rounded skull are from the Poodle.

Miniature Schnauzer

Miniature Poodle

Miniature Poodle

PAWS AND LEGS

The Poodle has small, oval feet, cushioned on thick pads. The Schnauzer has strong, straight legs set wide apart.

Miniature Schnauzer

EARS

These are mostly Schnauzer ears: high set, small, V-shaped and folding close to the skull. But the furriness comes from the Poodle.

Miniature Schnauzer

Miniature Poodle

The DOGnosis

Miniature Poodle

Miniature Schnauzer

Miniature Poodle

BODY

Short and deep, with a straight topline that declines slightly from the shoulders to the tail, like the Schnauzer's. Square body shape in profile, with a deep and moderately wide chest, like the Poodle's.

Miniature Schnauzer

Miniature Poodle

COAT

The double coat, with a wiry outercoat and softer undercoat, is like the Schnauzer's. That grey closer to the body is a Schnauzer colour underneath. But the hair is softer and longer than the Schnauzer's – that's the Poodle influence.

Miniature Schnauzer

Index

Resources

Books

Breed References
Complete Book of Dogs, Dog Breeds, and Dog Care, by Peter Larkin and Mike Stockman, Southwater, 2006.
The Kennel Club's Illustrated Breed Standards: The Official Guide to Registered Breeds, by The Kennel Club, Ebury Press, 2003.
New Encyclopedia of the Dog, 2nd Edition, by Bruce Fogle, DVM, Dorling Kindersley Publishers, 2002.

Dog Health, Care and Training
The Culture Clash, by Jean Donaldson, James & Kenneth Publishers, 1996.
Dog Manual: The Definitive Guide to Finding Your Perfect Dog, Training Him, and Having a Happy Life Together, by Carolyn Menteith, J H Haynes & Co, 2007.
The Truth About Dogs, by Stephen Budiansky, Phoenix Press, 2002.
What's Up with My Dog?, by Bruce Fogle, DVM, Dorling Kindersley Publishers, 2002.

Adoption Organisations

These are just a few of the bigger ones. You can find local shelters and adoption groups all over the country.

Battersea Dogs & Cats Home
020 7622 3626
www.dogshome.org

The Blue Cross
01993 822 651
www.bluecross.org.uk

Dogs Trust
0207 833 0006
www.dogstrust.org.uk

RSPCA
0870 0101 181
www.rspca.org.uk
Wood Green Animal Shelters
01480 832803
www.woodgreen.org.uk

Web Sites

The Kennel Club
www.thekennelclub.org.uk
Learn about purebred dogs and their physical make-up here.

Pet Health Council
www.pethealthcouncil.co.uk
The latest on veterinary care, and much more useful information, including nutrition, dealing with allergies and tips for international travel.

The Dog Rescue Pages
www.dogpages.org.uk
This site lists dogs available for adoption all over the U.K. It also includes a forum on dog training.

Picture Credits

Mutts photographed by Marc Henrie: 5, 16, 18, 22, 16, 30, 34, 38, 42, 46–177; Back Cover, Front Flap, Back Flap

Front Matter and Part 1 Mutts
6 SS/Jennifer Sekerka; 8 SS/Robert J. Daveant; 9 BSP/Nicole Hrustyk; 10 SS/Jiri Vaclavek; 11 JI; 25 JI

Purebreds
Affenpinscher JI 33, 36, 50, 51
Airedale Terrier SS/vnlit 23, 24, 32, 34, 37, 62, 63, 68, 69, 72, 73
Akita (sitting) wiki/Dante Alighieri 31, 32, 93
Akita (standing) JI 39, 40, 43, 45, 93, 100, 101
Australian Cattle Dog (sitting) SS/Curt Pickens 19, 20, 138
Australian Cattle Dog (standing) SS/Stas Volik 13, 32, 35, 36, 138, 139
Australian Shepherd (sitting) wiki/Pleple2000 152, 153
Australian Shepherd (standing) SS/Iztok Noc 25, 31, 33, 81
Australian Terrier (sitting) SS/Pixshots 51, 76
Australian Terrier (standing) SS/Pixshots 34, 36, 51, 76, 77
Basenji SS/Magdalena Szachowska 13
Basset Hound (sitting) SS/Eric Isselée 19, 20, 33, 36. 42, 112, 113, 154, 155
Basset Hound (standing) Star Media Ltd. 45, 155
Beagle (adult) BSP/Frank-Peter Funke 19, 20, 39, 41, 42, 44, 82, 118, 137, 156, 182, 183
Beagle (puppy) SS/Eric Isselée 31, 33, 83, 112, 113, 118, 136, 137, 143, 156, 157, 182, 183
Bearded Collie (black and white) BSP/Jessica Bilén 32, 35, 36, 44, 153
Bearded Collie (grey and white) SS/Eric Isselée 90, 91, 152, 153
Beauceron SS/Eric Isselée 28, 29, 35, 37, 80, 81, 130, 131
Border Collie (profile) Kent Dannen 36, 90, 91, 98, 100, 115
Border Collie (three-quarters) SS/Andra? Cerar 99, 100, 101, 114, 115
Border Terrier Kent Dannen 21, 23, 24, 31, 33, 41, 58, 59, 60, 61, 66, 72, 73
Borzoi (lying) BSP/Alexandr Anastasin 13
Borzoi (standing) BSP/Alexandr Anastasin 24, 27, 28, 39, 41, 44, 120, 121, 126, 127
Boxer BSP/Eric Isselée 33, 43, 44, 52, 53, 64, 65, 70, 71, 74, 75, 88, 89, 94, 168, 169
Brittany wiki/JL GOASDOUE 28, 37,45,114,115,144,145
Bulldog SS/Eric Isselée 24, 25, 27, 29, 34, 43, 45, 64, 65
Bullmastiff (sitting) SS/Marilyn Barbone 64, 65, 74, 86, 169
Bullmastiff (standing) Kent Dannen 27, 29, 43, 45, 75, 86, 87, 168, 169
Cairn Terrier (lying) wiki/Kathrin Albrecht 29, 45, 50, 51, 58, 60, 61
Cairn Terrier (sitting) wiki/Ronald Müller-Hagen 20, 50, 51, 59
Canadian Inuit Dog wiki/Mr.sparkle1 12
Carolina Dog wiki/Riverside Rescue 13
Cavalier King Charles Spaniel (sitting) SS/Elaine Hudson 149
Cavalier King Charles Spaniel (standing) SS/Dusan Po 37, 41, 148, 149
Chesapeake Bay Retriever Kent Dannen 20, 40, 44, 160, 161, 176, 177
Chihuahua (lying) SS/Mike Ludkowski 20, 32, 134, 140, 151
Chihuahua (sitting) wiki/Schenk fotos 135, 141, 150, 151
Chihuahua (standing) BSP/Emmanuelle Bonzami 135, 141, 151
Cocker Spaniel (sitting) SS/Karla Caspari 184, 185
Cocker Spaniel (standing) BSP/Jozsef Tibor 20, 44, 184, 185
Collie (profile) Kent Dannen 25, 84, 85, 96, 97, 98, 99, 100, 101, 114, 177
Collie (three-quarters) SS/Waldemar Dabrowski 19, 21, 23, 84, 85, 97, 99, 101, 115, 177
Corgi (sitting) SS/Annette 20, 36, 82, 83, 112, 113, 138, 139, 144
Corgi (standing) BSP/Cindy Haggerty 28, 82, 139, 145

Dachshund SS/Kuzma 27, 28, 39, 41, 43, 45, 136, 137, 142, 143, 144, 145, 154, 155
Dalmation SS/WizData, inc. 31, 32, 35, 37, 164, 165
Dandie Dinmont Terrier Kent Dannen 28, 58, 59
Doberman Pinscher SS/Yuri Arcurs 25, 27, 29, 33, 37, 43, 45, 96, 97, 130, 131
English Setter Kent Dannen 37, 165, 174, 175
English Springer Spaniel Star Media Ltd. 24, 37, 43, 45, 123
Finnish Lapphund wiki/Pleple2000 24, 36, 43, 44, 45, 80, 81
Finnish Spitz Kent Dannen 25, 40, 56, 57, 87, 147
Flat-Coated Retriever Kent Dannen 32, 35, 36, 43, 44, 171
Foxhound Kent Dannen 20, 30, 118, 119, 122, 123, 160, 161, 170
French Bulldog SS/ingret 19, 20, 23, 25, 28, 36, 156, 157
German Shepherd (profile) PhotoDisc, Inc. 30, 35, 37, 82, 83, 89, 94, 95, 96, 97, 102, 103, 176, 177
German Shepherd (three-quarters) Brand X Pictures 39, 41, 82, 88, 96
German Shorthaired Pointer BSP/Larry Gibason 35, 37, 41, 110, 111, 164
Golden Retriever SS/Lisa A. Svara 24, 85, 92, 93, 166, 176, 177
Great Dane SS/Eric Isselée 27, 29, 35, 37, 39, 40, 45, 75, 124, 125, 172, 173, 174, 175
Greater Swiss Mountain Dog Kent Dannen 36, 38, 40, 98, 99, 157
Greyhound wiki/Scott Feldstein/Creative Commons Attribution License 2.0 13, 20, 28, 32, 35, 37, 108, 109, 119, 121, 124, 125, 126, 127, 128, 129, 130, 131, 165, 166, 167, 172, 173
Hamiltonstovare Carol Ann Johnson 20, 122, 123, 160, 161
Ibizan Hound IO/Ralph Reinhold 13, 27, 29, 35, 37, 41, 106, 107, 108, 109, 116, 117, 127
Irish Terrier (lying) PhotoDisc, Inc. 54, 68, 80, 116
Irish Terrier (running) SS/Claudia Steininger 33, 36, 54, 69, 116, 117
Irish Water Spaniel (black) Kent Dannen 32, 129
Irish Water Spaniel (brown) wiki/Pleple2000 129
Irish Wolfhound (profile) Kent Dannen 117
Irish Wolfhound (three-quarters) IO/Ralph Reinhold 13, 25, 29, 110, 111, 116, 117
Jack Russell Terrier BSP/Eric Isselée 35, 36, 134, 135, 136, 137, 141, 142, 143, 148, 149
Keeshond Kent Dannen 24, 33, 146, 147
Labrador Retriever SS/Johanna Goodyear 29, 33, 39, 40, 43, 44, 86, 87, 98, 110, 111, 142, 143, 160, 161, 162, 163, 166, 167, 168, 169, 170, 171, 180, 181
Lakeland Terrier Kent Dannen 21, 38, 54, 55, 67, 68, 69
Malamute (sitting) StockExchange: Iza Oblak 12, 29, 44, 102
Malamute (standing) wiki/Klaus Helgert 40, 80, 81, 102
Malinois (in water) SS/Laila Kazakevica 84, 88, 89, 96
Malinois (lying) BSP/Sergejs Nescereckis 24
Malinois (profile) BSP/Emmanuelle Bonzami 84, 85, 88
Manchester Terrier Kent Dannen 32, 37, 41, 45, 56, 62, 63, 70, 71, 106, 107, 134, 135, 137, 156, 157
Miniature Pinscher (lying) BSP/Randy Harris 31, 33, 44, 77, 135, 139
Miniature Pinscher (standing) BSP/Anke van Wyk 135
Miniature Poodle Kent Dannen 152, 153, 184, 185, 186, 187
Miniature Schnauzer SS/Waldemar Dabrowski 72, 73, 186, 187
Norfolk Terrier Kent Dannen 21, 33, 57, 60, 61, 76, 77
Norwegian Buhund Kent Dannen 13, 20, 86, 87, 92, 93
Norwegian Elkhound Kent Dannen 31, 33, 44, 89
Papillon BSP/Chris Blaisdell 33, 37, 43, 44, 148, 149
Peruvian Inca Orchid Alicia Ward 12
Petit Basset Griffon Vendeen wiki/Pleple2000 35, 36, 41, 90, 91
Pointer wiki/Peter Firus 23, 29, 40, 124, 125, 172, 173, 174, 175
Pomeranian Kent Dannen 24, 33, 39, 40, 146, 147, 150, 151
Pug (lying) Star Media Ltd. 21

Pug (standing) SS/Ferenc Szelepcsenyi 13, 25, 27, 28, 40, 45, 140, 141, 150, 151, 155, 182, 183
Rhodesian Ridgeback (lying) SS/Digital Multimedia Creations 24, 29, 119
Rhodesian Ridgeback (standing) SS/Deborah Aronds 19, 20, 87, 118, 119
Rottweiler SS/Rhonda Odonnell 23, 24, 29, 37, 102, 103, 130
Saluki Kent Dannen 20, 23, 24, 28, 29, 41, 108, 109, 120, 121
Scottish Deerhound (dark grey) Kent Dannen 27, 28, 33, 110. 111, 120, 121, 128
Scottish Deerhound (light grey) wiki/Pleple2000/Creative Commons Attribution ShareAlike license 2.5 110. 111, 120, 121, 128
Scottish Terrier Kent Dannen 23, 25, 51, 58, 59
Shar-Pei (lying) PhotoDisc, Inc. 155
Shar-Pei (standing) BSP/Eric Isselée 19, 21, 29, 32, 154
Shiba Inu (sitting) SS/Nicholas James Homrich 56, 146, 147
Shiba Inu (standing) Kent Dannen 13, 23, 24, 31, 32, 33, 57, 147
Siberian Husky SS/Jeffrey Ong Guo Xiong 19, 33, 39, 40, 44, 166, 167
Smooth Fox Terrier Kent Dannen 45, 52, 53, 56, 57, 122, 123
Soft Coated Wheaten Terrier Kent Dannen 25, 27, 55
Staffordshire Bull Terrier wiki/Dante Alighieri 19, 21, 24, 29, 31, 32, 40, 52, 53, 64, 65, 70, 71, 94, 95
Standard Poodle SS/Racheal Grazias 31, 32, 33, 39, 40, 129, 180, 181
Swedish Lapphund Carol Ann Johnson 150, 151
Tervuren Kent Dannen 41, 92, 93, 102
Tibetan Spaniel Kent Dannen 21, 25, 138, 140, 141
Vizla (sitting) wiki/Raquel Barousse 95
Vizla (standing) SS/Christine Nichols 36, 73, 94, 161, 162, 163
Weimaraner Morguefile/JJM 33, 162, 163, 170
Welsh Terrier Kent Dannen 37, 62, 63, 66, 67, 68, 69, 76, 77
Whippet (lying) SS/Magdalena Szachowska 19, 106, 109, 115, 122, 126, 163
Whippet (sitting) JI 39, 41
Whippet (standing) StockExchange/Cezar Perelles 20, 24, 28, 29, 32, 37, 84, 106, 107, 108, 109, 114, 115, 122, 123, 127, 162
Wire Fox Terrier Kent Dannen 25, 31, 32, 41, 54, 63, 66
Xoloitzcuintli Kent Dannen 12
Yorkshire Terrier (lying) SS/Joy Fera 61, 153
Yorkshire Terrier (standing) SS/Jackson Gee 27, 29, 60, 152

Designer Dogs
Cockapoo Chelle Calbert
Labradoodle Derek Ramsey/Creative Commons Attribution ShareAlike 2.5 License
Puggle SS/Rick's Photography
Schnoodle SS/Scott Bolster

Cover
Digital Vision Ltd.

JI: Jupiterimages Corporation
SS: ShutterStock
IO: IndexOpen
wiki: Wikipedia Commons
BSP: BigStockPhoto

David Alderton, Marc Henrie, and Hylas Publishing would like to thank Katie Cowan of Collins & Brown, an imprint of Anova Books, and Clarissa Baldwin, Beverly Price, Chris Slight, Richard Moore, Sandra Wilson, Alison Rodger, Dianne Porter, Eleanor Silk and the staff of Dogs Trust.